When Horses Fly

An Allegorical Melodrama

by

Blaine Turner

When Horses Fly
An Allegorical Melodrama

ISBN 978-0-578-14952-3

Cover photo: Dani Crabtree
Photo page 2: Casey Sperling
Photos page 11 & 12: Kathryn Krause
Drawings pages 32, 63 & 85: Joseph Janga
Photo page 39: Caroline Baca
Numerous Horse photos: Jeanna Colombo
Other photos and drawings by permission

From bulldogging to cat fighting,
this small-town rodeo is fertile ground
for cultivating high drama—
young love, sin and sacrifice.
Mildly allegorical, here the Bride of Christ
grapples with age-old questions
from the Beatitudes,
the Armor of God,
and the Seven Churches in Revelation.

Habakkuk 1:8

Their horses are swifter
than leopards,
fiercer than wolves at dusk.
Their cavalry gallops headlong;
their horsemen come
from afar.
They fly like an eagle
swooping to devour

New International Version

Matthew 5

Introduction to the
Sermon on the Mount

[1] Now when Jesus saw the crowds, he went up on a mountainside and sat down. His disciples came to him, [2] and he began to teach them.

The Beatitudes

He said:

[3] "Blessed are the poor in spirit,
for theirs is the kingdom of heaven.
[4] Blessed are those who mourn,
for they will be comforted.
[5] Blessed are the meek,
for they will inherit the earth.
[6] Blessed are those who hunger and thirst for
righteousness, for they will be filled.
[7] Blessed are the merciful,
for they will be shown mercy.
[8] Blessed are the pure in heart,
for they will see God.
[9] Blessed are the peacemakers,
for they will be called children of God.
[10] Blessed are those who are persecuted because of
righteousness, for theirs is the kingdom of heaven.

[11] "Blessed are you when people insult you,
persecute you and falsely say all kinds of evil
against you because of me. [12] Rejoice and be glad,
because great is your reward in heaven, for in the
same way they persecuted the prophets who were
before you.

New International Version

Acts 17:29

[29] "Therefore since we are God's offspring, we should not think that the divine being is like gold or silver or stone—an image made by human design and skill.

New International Version

1 Peter 1:18-19

[18] For you know that it was not with perishable things such as silver or gold that you were redeemed from the empty way of life handed down to you from your ancestors, [19] but with the precious blood of Christ, a lamb without blemish or defect.

New International Version

Dedicated to all horse lovers, but remember …

Psalm 33:17-20

¹⁷ A horse is a vain hope for deliverance;
   despite all its great strength it cannot save.
¹⁸ But the eyes of the LORD are on those who fear him,
   on those whose hope is in his unfailing love,
¹⁹ to deliver them from death
   and keep them alive in famine.

²⁰ We wait in hope for the LORD;
   he is our help and our shield.

New International Version

When Horses Fly
An Allegorical Melodrama

Chapter 1
The Parade

"Wake up! A rodeo! A Rodeo came to town last night!" All the kids were yelling at once! Yes, there were RVs and pickups and horse trailers parked all over, straddling curbs and violating lawns. Big rubber tires ground ruts in the grass. The streets were jammed. Children ran wild. Dogs broke chains. Bulls raged. Girls chewed gum and blew bubbles. Boys stuck theirs under benches. Rude noise blasted everywhere. What clown could be responsible for such all-fired fuss and flusteration?

The very air was exciting to breathe with whiffs of cattle and coffee stirring the innards. God was definitely shaking things up. Tall, muscular cowboys could be seen strutting about in big boots and bigger, magnificent wild-west hats which all but blocked the sun. They even wore them *indoors*, but no one seemed to mind. It was part of the show. Ten gallon Stetsons, some black, some brown, some white—all of them fresh, fancy and fetching. Galón means colorful braids but the hatbands here were tooled leather. Hotdog hawkers scampered beneath the wide brims like pigeons under picnic umbrellas.

The colorful braids were on the girls. Many had ribbons flowing through them. It was the first day of rodeo, and a time for horseplay with pony-tails—a time for sweethearts, sweet-tooth and sweet-clover. Such things spirit joy on breezes and swirl with dust to tickle knees and noses. Color splashes rampant over children's balloons to pour onto bright smiling faces. Pink cotton candy drifts about on sticks, making every cheek and nose sticky sweet. Girls pull their hair away and lick bubblegum lips. Boys squint around corners at them and finger cap pistols. The sun sees all and blesses the morning, but there are always clouds crouching just behind the horizon?

As the program starts, the bleachered crowd begins clapping and cheering at the parade of fancy-chapped cowgirls, shapely astride their sleek and stately horses. The majestic animals trot, prance and gallop, shaking their splendid heads at the wind. Long, wild girl-hair and luxurious horse-manes toss together in the breeze, as loose turf thunders by underneath. Flags soar everywhere to signal the start of the greatest show anywhere, and every child's breast is bursting with anticipation.

Crimany—the angelicas! God's finest handiwork. How lovely they looked carrying their lofty flags that brisk autumn day! How thrilling! Eight of them. Magnificent angels, but the sweetest by far was neither the fanciest, nor the most glamorous, nor even the bravest rider. She was smaller than the rest. And younger. She rode last in line and collected most of the dust. Her clothes, never fancy to begin with, were now absolutely threadbare, and there was an obvious tear in one elbow. Her hat had blown off and rested ingloriously against the far fence. When the girls halted and turned to salute the crowd, all gazes rested on this woeful, innocent face and childlike countenance. "Blessed are the poor in spirit," everyone must have thought as she tried her best to blink dirt out of her big, wide-set eyes.

She didn't wave or grin broadly to the people like the other cowgirls. They were also young beauties, to be sure, but more like fillies rode hard and put away wet. Underneath the dust, this girl resembled an impish pixie more than a rodeo princess. Her long-lashed eyes were playful, yet on her brow were etched persistent lines of disquiet. She herself could never put a finger on it, but it pressed on her heart and squeezed tears down her cheeks. At times it made her mouth dry and her throat ache. "Blessed are those who mourn," was all she could think of at such times. She longed for the full peace of God, whatever that could be.

But she lived in a naughty world of self-pleasure and sin. Nevertheless, she always tried to be a good girl. She thought of her soul as originally snow white but now stained on the edges with the urinations of rude rodeo animals (referred to in these parts as men). So in the parade she didn't slap her thighs or provocatively toss dust from her hair. She was different. She didn't bat eyelashes at the boys in the bleachers. No, not at all. She didn't use swear words and wouldn't listen to them either. She refused makeup and hair coloring. Her locks were naturally curly, not made with hot irons. She didn't drink, smoke, chew gum or hang on the cowboys and their every word—the worthless corral dust used to impress women. She wouldn't laugh at crude jokes or sit in dark theaters with men. She wouldn't even shake bare hands with them, she decided. She tried to keep her soul as white as possible, but its edges became frayed nevertheless.

Maybe this was what made her so bashful. So shy in fact, that no one even knew her name. Everyone just called her Curlygirl because of the long blond hair which hung about her creamy face in bouncy swirls. She was so timid that ordinary people could hardly speak to her. When they did, she would always turn her head and her big blue eyes would never meet theirs. "Blessed are the meek," she would reflect inwardly.

So there she sat, sweetly on her pony, gently fingering an ornate crucifix adorning her slender neck. It was solid silver and lay precious against her skin—a figurine of the only man in her life. She often touched it when she was alone in her trailer. Highly polished from the prints of her fingering, it was the one thing in her world that seemed to return love. She idolized it. It was dear to her.

All too soon the parade reached its breath-defying climax with eight bejeweled cowboys thundering about the arena in line from tallest to smallest. Men. Images of God, yes of mighty gods. Around and around they sped, burning the breeze with colossal steeds under their thighs.

They rode like greased lightning, swifter than the girls and more power-fully. Exciting men. Their shoulders were broad and their hips hard and narrow. Their spurs spun in the sun. As the crowd clapped and cheered, they reined in their mounts to inter-weave into the waiting rank of cow-girls. Each girl was straining to hold her enormous silk flag erect and splendid ready. The crowd could hardly contain themselves. They screamed and pounded boots into the benches, making an awful ruckus.

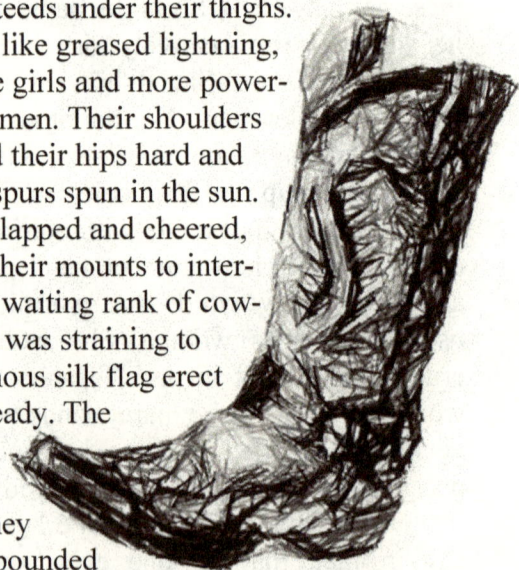

The first cowboy in line was the largest, most sturdily built, and most fun to look at by far. "A real bulldozer," twittered the gum-snapping tweenie-babes. They all called him "Hubba Bubba Buck." He called them his "Chiclets," and would carry them around on his biceps three and four at a time. Of all the cowhands, his shoulders were the broadest and his hips the most firm and finely sculptured. His teeth were the whitest. His face was chiseled from Italian marble and his craggy hands were Montana granite. In addition, he was the most highly endowed with self-assurance. Positively puffed with pride, you could say. Gallant and erect. It was plain as day he was the biggest toad in the pond.

So it was not surprising that he should roughly jerk his great white stallion to stand squarely beside, and even nudge little Curlygirl as she sat her diminutive pinto mare. The big cowboy's nostrils flared like those of his horse, and his arm waved grandly to the crowd. He made an imposing show of tipping his hat and giving a knowing wink to the long-haired brunette on his left. She had warm golden skin but the look she shot back was cold steel. She was a pistol—aimed at his ample chest. So he swayed the other way in the saddle to inquire with a commanding flourish, "Will ya come tuh the dance tonight, Juicy Fruit? Come a tie yai yippy kai yea."

Shocked as always, Curlygirl released her cross and averted her eyes. A blush appeared, even through the dust on her cheek. Her flag, however, remained tall and her horse stood its ground.

"I'll trot with you at a dance when horses fly," she muttered, then added under her breath, "Blessed are the weak, for they will inherit the earth." She thought about complaining to the owner of the rodeo, but nobody knew who it was. Why would such a person remain in hiding? Buck seemed to be running the show. Instead of thinking about yippy kai yea, she rested her mind on precious times with her silver crucifix and stroking her handsome tooled leather Bible waiting by her bedside. Branded on it were three stylized crosses atop a hill with winding streams running down. Also her Jesus was majestically emblazoned in one corner. He was a brown bust resembling Tarzan, with strong features well-oiled by soft, adoring hands. The gilt-edged pages inside him were white, crisp and unblemished as snow. He was a pure, dear white lamb and knew and loved her in a personal way like no one else. He just perfectly filled the God-shaped hole in her heart. He was the answer to all her questions and the fulfillment of all her dreams.

But oh how he made her suffer. She cried when she thought of him languishing there on that wood, wrist-nailed by those terrible torturing men. While hammering they had been so careful not to tear his blood vessels; now they were laughing and swearing—crude smelly men with big arms, small eyes and missing teeth. They had whipped him and taunted him and fooled around with his clothes. A garland of long, sharp thorns chewed mockingly into his head, with blood trickling down. Curlygirl wanted to wipe it away but his friends crouched back in fear, as did she. The soldiers eyed her. The air was rancid, hot and still. Even the sun was awful, as it hung for hours above the Son of Man, hung naked under its rays.

This and worse, just to offer the hand of rescue to all the spiritually dead who would submit to be drawn to him, even when they could not come under their own power. Yes the hand reached out even to this blemished bloom of Eve with the cute button nose—this, the blossom who now comes to him every day and carries him around on her neck and precious in her heart.

Then his side was stabbed and he mumbled something, cried out and expired right under everyone's agonized gaze. "Today you will be with me in Paradise," she had heard. Curlygirl just knew his words were for her.

After that there were the groans of rough spikes being wrenched from blood-soaked wood—the wretched spectacle of a lifeless body brought down—reverently, but with dead flesh quivering red like butcher meat handled until growing stiff in a mother's arms. Then ashen faces pleading down into a cold, vacant one—too much for any mind to bear. And Curlygirl was there in the eerie darkness. Her eyes became wet for him and her throat dry. Her stomach churned and her forearms ached. She wanted to hold him herself and blot away all the stain from his inert body. So she did. And soon she well and truly had his blood on her hands. His blood covered her. Even today his appearance would be shocking. (*Revelation 5:6*)

She suffered so. Now she was distraught that her Jesus was not with her to biff Buck in his chiseled nose. Neither was he here to sweep her up in his arms, kiss her forehead and whisk her away to… Well she didn't even know where he lived, this only man in her life. Not in outer space she hoped. Yeah Paradise, but where might that be? "Blessed are those who mourn," she thought, "for they will be comforted. So, bring it on! But how exactly?"

As a second-rate cowgirl she had nothing to offer him, nothing to show for her life except hair. What would he want with curly hair, a puny pony, a broken-down pickup and a dilapidated bunk house horse trailer? Well she did have her purity. She had that for Jesus. That and 186 dollars and 67 cents. It was like she didn't have a tail feather left. Yet "blessed are the poor," she had to reflect, "for theirs is the kingdom of heaven. But when? So hurry up, if you please." Oh the daydreams she had.

Now the last cowboy to fall in line was not as tall as Buck, certainly not as muscular, and definitely not as exciting to look at. He was experienced, but a newbie to this particular rodeo. This last cowboy couldn't afford any of the fancy dancy outfits that adorned the others. His hat was decidedly smaller, really a baseball cap, and his boots resembled old hiking shoes. The seat of his pants was worn thin by saddle leather. He looked like a tumbleweed.

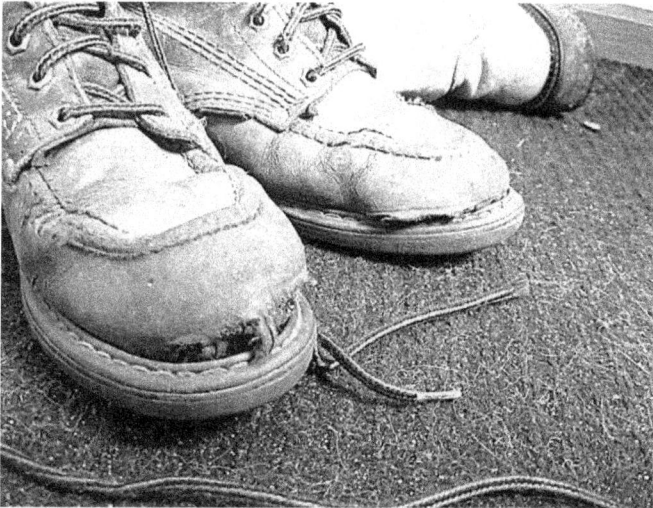

Because of this, he was more than a little shy, and no one even knew his name. Everyone just called him "Ponyboy," not just because of his small horse, but because of his own pint size. He was so shy in fact, that ordinary people could hardly even talk to him. When they did, he would always turn his head slightly and his big brown eyes would never meet theirs. He would glance self-consciously down to the old scuffed-leather Bible which was constantly in his hand. Scratched as it was on the outside, it was so worn on the inside as to be almost in tatters. Many pages were stained, some torn and taped, and almost all marked with pencils and pens of various inks. "Blessed are those who hunger and thirst for righteousness," you might say, "for they will be filled."

This was Ponyboy. The cowboys sometimes called him "Punyboy" to see if they could get his dander up. But he never got mad. Even though they considered him young, between hay and grass, it was hard to actually make fun of him because of his pony. Yes, what his pony lacked in size, it more than made up in skill and cunning. It was indeed the best schooled rodeo horse anyone had ever seen. Some even called it mystifying the way it could maneuver its rider into position to rope a calf or wrestle a steer. Ponyboy, in fact, attributed his modest success on the rodeo circuit, not to his own meager skills, but to the astonishing abilities of his beloved horse. Ultimate credit, of course went to the God of his dog-eared Bible, who seemed to take a personal interest in him. Or so he claimed. Just the other day he was reading in *Philippians 4:13, "I can do all this through him who gives me strength. (NIV)."* When teased he would just shy away and quote things like that, which only served to spur on his antagonizers.

"Blessed are the pure in heart," he would think quietly, "for they will see God." Ponyboy knew that he was chosen for salvation by a sovereign God, and as far as he knew, this made him unique in all the rodeo world. And therefore special. And in the only aspect that really matters, superior.

Not that he was chosen on the basis of his own merit, he knew that. He was just a shave-tail dunderhead—no great shucks. But God has his own plans and Ponyboy was grateful to be riding with him as his lowly cowhand.

Lowly cowhand or not, Ponyboy had one glaring weakness which neither his horse, nor his Bible seemed able to fix. It had nothing to do with the rodeo competition, the quality of his clothes, or even his religion. It was this: Even though he was new, he was already soft down on Curlygirl. Hopelessly. Not physically so much, he tried to rationalize, but sorry for her obvious loneliness. Still, she was pretty as a speckled pup and when it came to true love he'd been in the desert so long, he knew all the lizards by their first names. "Blessed are the merciful," he reflected, "for they will be shown mercy." So he was sweet on her. And truth be known, it probably *was* a physical attraction after all. All cowboy blood runs red, doesn't it? She was his truelove girl.

After the parade she was the first to exit the arena, with Buck close at her heels. Ponyboy was last and on a whim he broke ranks and circled over to retrieve Curlygirl's hat which had blown over against the fence. He galloped by and leaned down without dismounting. Too bad she couldn't have seen it. But another rider did— circling back to gaze over the fence at him.

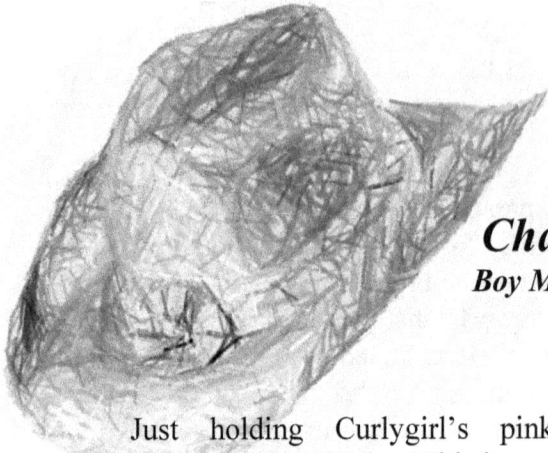

Chapter 2
Boy Meets Girl

Just holding Curlygirl's pink hat made Ponyboy's fingers tingle. With its cute red ribbon bow it seemed small and precious in his hands. He looked for her, but by the time he'd put his horse away she was long gone into her trailer. He longed for her.

Not that she ever noticed him, he assumed. None of the girls had. In fact none of the girls noticed anyone but Buck. Even the wide-hipped buckle bunnies who followed the trailers had eyes only for him. Buck was so this and so that and so everything wonderful. His horse was so this and so that and so everything amazing. Even his hat was, well you get the picture. A perfect ten gallons. And Buck was so good at noticing girls back, at one time or another they all became quite fully smitten with him. All of them, that is, except Curlygirl, who never noticed anyone back—outwardly anyway. She would just caress that cross around her neck, turn it over and over in her fingers, and bow her head. This, of course drove Buck wild and he was constantly this and constantly that, showing off this, displaying that and endlessly bothering her. Yet she kept her eyes politely averted at all times and in the arena especially, kept her flag properly erect and proud.

"Blessed are those who are mistreated because of virtue, for theirs is the kingdom of heaven," she

16

purred under her breath. In times like these, her cross became reassuringly warm in her hands.

She would not speak to Buck even when he won the bareback riding contest one week. She would not speak to him when he won the bull riding contest the next week—or when he won both in the same week. She would not even speak to him when he began winning *every* week.

This was because, she hated to admit, while Buck was riding everything in sight, another cowboy began winning most of the contests involving teamwork between horse and man. "The horse makes the man," she always said, for she was guarding her heart for the best all-around horseman in the world. Not that she was eaten up with hankering for this make-believe person. That would be sinful and she was a very devout, pious girl. "You don't have to attend church to be religious," she always thought. After all, her real man was always there for her, hanging around her neck on a cross. Dying for her. Yet she had to admit sometimes he seemed lifeless and stiff. He could never embrace her like the imaginary horseman. He couldn't put his arms around her and nibble her ear. He wouldn't whisper sweet suggestive nothings into her soul. Sure, Jesus could perish for her, but only her horseman would be able to live, ride and fistfight for her. But which horseman? Which was God's will for her? She must find the right one. And quick. Or would God just choose for her? That was probably it. Such were her ruminations.

Now take Ponyboy. He was sweet and quiet. And he didn't do well fighting anything that would buck him off, but he and that horse of his certainly teamed up well to chase things. He was fast as a jackrabbit and sleek as a fox—handsome as one too. Just because Curlygirl's eyes never lingered on men, didn't mean they failed to detect and reflect on manly accomplishments and characteristics. Would he ever want to chase *her*?

"Blessed are those who hunger and thirst, for they will be filled," she mused, moistening her lips.

And yet there was Buck—right before her eyes. Oh so big on his white horse and busting out a chute, chasing a small brown calf. His forearms, bigger than her thighs, were piercing the air like missiles. Then the great cowboy was swinging his stiff rope lariat in a big circle over his head. The powerful horse was thundering just at the heels of the awkward, terrified calf. Suddenly Buck flung the loop skillfully over its head and jerked his horse to a dead stop. The steed almost sat down in the dust. The rope choked taut and yanked the calf head over heels hard onto its back. For an agonizing moment it just lay there in the dirt, its neck bent back at a gruesome angle. When it tried to get up Buck's horse dragged it a few feet to keep the rope tight.

Meanwhile Buck had swung his left leg backwards over the saddle and just before it touched the ground, pulled his right boot from the stirrup. He hit the turf running, following the rope with his right, then left hand to the calf. He coaxed the rope slack to let the animal rise, then with all his might lifted it high into the air and slammed it back down into the dirt. A groan escaped from the crowd.

He then deftly tied the calf's right foreleg to both of its hind legs. Instantly he raised his hands high to stop the time clock and also to wave at the crowd. As he strutted around grinning and tipping his hat to everyone, his horse continued to drag the calf mercilessly through the dust. After a few moments the official time was posted – 10 seconds. Buck celebrated, chest protruding, and hot-dogged his horse on a victory lap before departing through a gate.

The calf rose bawling painfully and hobbled grotesquely around the arena like a half-squashed spider. A small amount of blood oozed from its nose and foam from its mouth. Quickly it was herded into a special enclosure where it staggered against a rail and was dragged inside a truck headed for slaughter. No painkillers were administered because, according to the rodeo veterinarian, "that ruins the meat."

Curlygirl smiled as the next man up was Ponyboy. The crowd hushed in anticipation as his name and number were called. Just then a vendor yelled "HOT DOG," and there was quiet laughter. Like Buck, Ponyboy positioned his horse at the back of a pen that had a rope barrier to bar entrance into the arena. Beside this pen was a chute with spring-loaded doors, containing a calf. A light, twenty-eight foot rope was tied around the calf's neck and attached to a trip lever which held the barrier rope in place. The barrier is used to make sure the calf gets a head start. On Ponyboy's signal the calf was released and it ran straight out into the open. When it had gone twenty-eight feet the rope pulled taut, tripping the lever, releasing the barrier and starting the time clock. The force of this broke the thin rope from the calf's neck and it began running free.

Ponyboy had timed things perfectly. His horse had started into its gallop just a split second before the barrier went down. This saved valuable time as they sped after the calf. Quickly the calf was lassoed, but unlike Buck, Ponyboy did not jerk it to the ground. This saved him more seconds as he easily flipped it onto its side. With a short rope carried in his teeth, he tied the three legs together using a half hitch he called "two wraps and a hooey." It took less than a second. During all this his horse kept the lasso rope taut but was careful not drag or strangle the calf.

When it was properly tied Ponyboy immediately went back to his horse and released the tension on the rope. As he was riding away his score was announced. Seven seconds. A winning time!

Whenever Ponyboy would win, there would be Curlygirl, peering around a corner or stealing sideways glances so the other girls wouldn't notice. She was beginning to sense an odd new feeling inside her that made her blush. Secretly she was beginning to want to run up to Ponyboy after a big win and… well, just hug him. "Oh my," she feared, "I could never do *that*!"

Ponyboy, on the other hand, had pictured doing *that* to Curlygirl every day. Not in public, mind you. He would often peek as she curried her horse, hung up her hat, or even just walked somewhere. Hat? He wondered what hat that could be, since he'd been too shy to return hers lost in the arena. It sat contentedly on the shelf by his bed. He was happy to have it there. Every night he would decide to give in to his heart and try to actually give it back. But then he'd have to actually speak to her. At least he could tell her his real name, he thought. At least they would be able to converse politely while feeding or grooming their horses. At least they would be able to say, "Hi" on the trails. And every day he would walk right past her, fearing even the slightest gesture or utterance would upset things. What things? Every day he would go on about his business as if she never existed, as if she was thin air. Yet incredibly, everyday as he walked past, Curlygirl would gaze at the big number 12 pinned to his back and make a silent wish, a fond one, which she supposed would never come true.

And every night her thoughts became more and more poetic. Alone in her trailer she would put on her playlist of Christian love songs which could apply equally to her Jesus and to her other man. The two became fused somehow and this made her dancing pure, holy and present in her mind. In her room she could dance and make it a prayer. She could be open and intimate. Yes, she danced as a lacewing, but only for him and never in front of a window. The way David danced, she told herself. But he was a man.   And Jesus would love her the way he created   her, all girl and after his own heart.

Then she fell asleep to these words:

"³As the apple tree among the trees of the wood, so is my beloved among the sons. I sat down under his shadow with great delight, and his fruit was sweet to my taste.

⁴He brought me to the banqueting house, and his banner over me was love.

⁵Stay me with flagons, comfort me with apples: for I am sick of love.

⁶His left hand is under my head, and his right hand doth embrace me."

Song of Solomon 2
King James Version

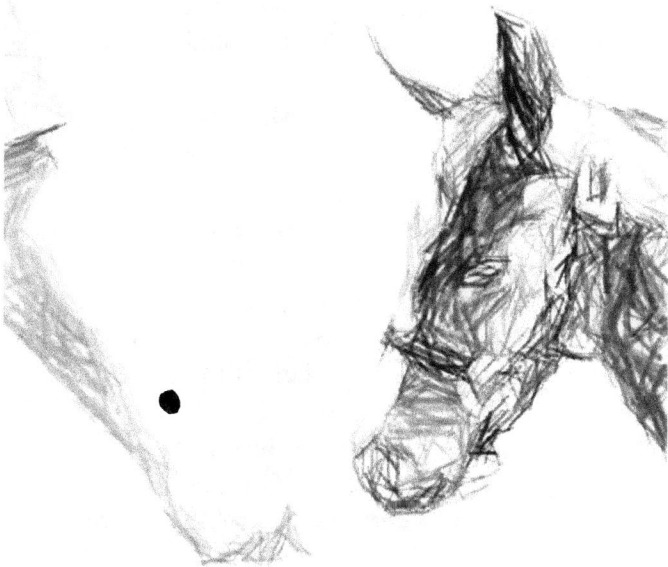

Late one evening such a reverie was interrupted by a timid knock at her door. Curlygirl guessed it one of her girlfriends because no man had set foot in her trailer since the air-conditioning was installed. So she slipped on a light robe and flung open the door, banging it into the face of a young man standing too close on the step.

"Oh I'm so sorry," she said, "Sir—I mean Ponyboy." He had fallen off the step, lost his hat and crushed the other one he was carrying.

Ponyboy! That handsome new dude. The object of private dreams. Curlygirl wanted to say come in and stay a while. Sit down. Stay a long time. Have a coke. Love me. Marry me. So she leaned out the door and said, "Ponyboy! What in the Sam Hill are you doing here at this hour?"

Ponyboy wanted to say that his heart was breaking so much for her that he couldn't stand up anymore. He wanted to hug and kiss her, but he was breathless. So he said, "Ah jis wanted to return your hat m... mm... ma'am."

They looked at the crushed hat together. He tried to fix it but only succeeded in pinching it even more out of shape.

"Well you'd better dust off and come in. We'll see what we can do," said Curlygirl. She opened the door wide and he stumbled up the steps. Inside there was only a small table, a bed and one chair. The boy thought it impolite to view her sitting on the bed, so he went over to it himself, but then awkwardly opted to perch on the edge of the chair.

"Would you like a coke?" she said, taking the smashed hat and nervously stroking it with her hands.

"Sure, that would be cool," he said.

"I don't have any ice," she said. "So now I suppose I can return that loaner hat." She glanced at the wall by the door, where it hung on a hook.

"Sorry," he said.

She brought him a coke bottle and sat on the bed with hers. She hastily, but casually threw a blanket over her pillow and carefully adjusted her robe. "Where'd you find it?" she asked.

"Oh you lost it in the arena," he said, avoiding her eyes.

"Sometime back…" she said. "I thought it was stolen."

He glanced around the room self-consciously. His eyes, afraid to rest on her body, circled at its edges and spied the pretty silver crucifix on the bedside table.

"Pretty," he said in mid-swallow, almost choking on the coke.

The girl blushed and stiffened. "What?"

"I mean your crucifix," he said. "I didn't mean—you." There was an awkward silence and he wanted to bolt for the door. He stared at the floor.

"Oh this is my Jesus, on the cross for me." She picked it up and handed it to him.

"Oh you're a Christian too," he exclaimed, turning it over and over in his fingers. He'd never actually held a cross with Jesus still on it. Something began feeling odd about it so he added, "You know Jesus is no longer on the cross…"

"Of course he's no longer on the cross," she responded, wrinkling her forehead, "he's here in my heart." She put her hand there tenderly.

The boy had another swig of coke and said, "Well the Bible says he's at the right hand of the Father."

"Um, please don't tell me what I know and feel," she replied evenly, pursing her lips slightly, "he's in my heart 'cuz I asked him there."

"It's in *Acts 2:33*. Do you have a Bible?" He eyed her skeptically.

"Of course I have a Bible, a really nice one. I take care of it." She opened the drawer in her nightstand and handed him the heavy book.

Ponyboy noticed with a hint of grimace that it was the King James Version. The girl saw this and rolled her eyes ever so slightly. They were both trying to be so polite, like sweet children opening Christmas presents but finding only clothes. He opened to *Acts 2:33* and handed it back.

"See how nice and white I keep my pages," she said. He raised his eyebrows and she glared at him.

"Go ahead and read it," he said.

She did so silently and then looked up. "It says right hand of **God**, not the **Father**."

"Same thing," he said.

"Then they should *say* it," she said, "and you should quote more accurately. Besides, God is everywhere. So Jesus can be in my heart! Right, Mister Smarty?"

Ponyboy just stared at her. How could someone so cute be so mean to him?

Curlygirl scowled back. How could someone so handsome be so insensitive to her?

They finished their cokes in silence and she was relieved to let him out without further conversation.

In spite of this it was not long before she found herself standing again on the first rung of a fence to watch Ponyboy. Yes, he was the only boy she had ever given a coke to. Too bad he turned out to be a jerk. Now here he was, strapping himself to the back of the largest, meanest and dirtiest bull you could ever imagine. Yes bull CB635 weighed over a ton and was named Rufus. He could kill a man quick as look at him. There was evil in his one big black eye. He'd mangled a poor boy's arm and put his horn through several other fellows. Bad luck for Ponyboy; nobody had ever successfully ridden this bull. Cowboys considered themselves lucky to just get away without being gored or trampled. In fact they would say, "The only good reason to ride that bull would be to meet a hot nurse."

If anybody should ride Rufus, well he'd be champion for sure. You see, a good bucking bull gives a cowboy lots of points—if he can stay on for eight seconds that is. "Maybe Buck could," thought Curlygirl, "sure, he could!" But he'd never drawn that particular bull. What a contest it would be. Muscle on muscle, man against monster. "Buck could," she thought again, gripping the fence with her slender fingers, "he's so large and powerful. He could ride anything. He could clamp his massive legs behind that big bull hump and last for eight seconds easy. And he's mighty handsome too. But what did that have to do with it? Well a lot, apparently," her mind told her. She flushed a little and pulled her hat brim down a bit over her forehead. It was the very same hat that another cowboy had handled fondly, she reflected.

But wait! There was the gate swinging open and black Rufus hurling and spinning out of control into the arena. Yet it was number 12, not Buck, clinging desperately to his back. The boy looked thin and limp. The bull was thick and hard. Ponyboy was swinging his one free arm wildly in a vain attempt to keep his balance. The bull bounded and leaped high off the ground. Then it began bucking and twirling, faster and wilder. After just two seconds poor Ponyboy was thrown clean into the air as the crazed animal spun out from under him. Around and around whirled the big bull and to Curlygirl's horror, there was her Ponyboy, his hand still strapped tight—caught fast under the bull rope. It was a dreadful hang-up. His feet dangled limp on the ground. Around and around Rufus lunged, trying to dislodge the hated clinging creature lashed to his side. In a rage, he trampled the man's hat deep into the dust.

Ponyboy, tossed about like a filthy rag, appeared to have fainted. "Surely his wrist will break," thought Curlygirl with a gripping pain in her stomach. "Surely his feet will be trampled as he hangs there, half under the monster. He'll be kicked in the head. Surely I'm going to be sick!"

To be sure, Ponyboy would have died that day had it not been for a clown named Truth. This clown, actually the brave man underneath the baggy clothes, had instantly stopped being funny and literally threw himself into the path of the bull. He actually grabbed a horn and swinging on it, tried to pull Ponyboy's hand from the killer bull rope. As Rufus tossed the clown high in the air, the man managed to free the lashed hand and both landed ingloriously among the deadly dancing hooves. With uncanny strength the clown flung Ponyboy over his shoulder and staggered to safety behind a fence where they both collapsed in a heap. The bull was herded into his proper enclosure and the gate slammed reassuringly shut.

Only then did the crowd sit down, but continued buzzing like bees on wax. Truth stayed with Ponyboy until he came to and then sat with him on the fence for a while. "Close call, that," he said.

"The Lord was with me, for sure," said Ponyboy.

"Do you believe God does this sort of thing?" asked the clown.

"Of course," Ponyboy answered immediately, "I'm a true Christian. 'You have rescued me from the horns of the wild oxen!'"

"Oh, think nothing of it. It's Jesus who really saves lives."

"I know that," said Ponyboy, "I was quoting from *Psalm 22:21*. I know lots of verses about cows and horses."

The clown also knew a lot about cows and horses. He was what's called a "Protection Bullfighter." They compete for points displaying skill in conducting the bull rider to safety once his ride is over. The show isn't finished until the bull is herded out of the arena.

"I'm glad you know the Bible," said the clown, "say, do you know there's a little study in my trailer many evenings at seven? Why don't you come?"

"I thought I wasn't invited," came the shy reply. His real reason was that he feared the doctrine would be haywire in a rodeo Bible study.

"Aww shucks! Everyone is invited to a Bible study, always."

"Well maybe I will," Ponyboy said, but inwardly he was afraid to recite verses and pray before prying, judging eyes. And he would never have the courage to go alone.

"Who comes?" he asked.

"Just a few folks," said the clown.

Ponyboy's heart sank. He knew if he ever did go he would want to hide in the back of a big room with Curlygirl. But who was he kidding? "What are you studying?"

"The Beatitudes," said the clown. "We're just starting. Bring your girl if you want."

Ponyboy laughed inwardly.

Curlygirl hung on the fence until Ponyboy was safe from his bull. She never did throw up, but ached to rush over to him and tend to his wrist. Every bone inside her yearned to embrace his bruised body. But she didn't. She was too shy. And she was mad at him. She tried to remember why. He was a jerk?

Yet nothing could keep Ponyboy out of her mind. All cowgirl blood runs red, doesn't it? She strained to keep such thoughts private. It was her way. And Ponyboy never spoke to her either—not since that night in the trailer.

Not so with Buck. Yes, everyday, there he was chatting her up and fondly stroking her horse's neck or fondling its mane. It was his way. Unknown to her, in his pocket, among his loose jewels which he often displayed to the girls, was an engagement ring with a diamond rock wedged proudly in it. No one knew how or why he got it. Some say he just found it under some bleachers. It was shamefully big and bright. It brought him luck, he always boasted. And who could know **when** or upon **whom** he might be able to use such a thing to advantage? He thought he was so smart but *"wisdom is more valuable than gold and crystal. It cannot be purchased with jewels mounted in fine gold." Job 28:17 (NLT)*

Still Ponyboy pined for Curlygirl. And still they never spoke so much as a word. He thought about the times in the old bunkhouse when Buck was bragging about his ring to all the cowhands. He said it could make any girl sit up and beg. Wiggle it in the sunlight, he said, and it would make her drool. Give it as a gift, well then she'd do any doggone doggie trick he wished.

"Could this be true?" muttered Ponyboy to himself. He thought about this possibility quite often and these reflections built up in his mind like water behind a dam. He wished he could wash his mind out with soap, but decided God would have to do that. So he did—eventually, and in his way.

Chapter 3
The Bible Study

One evening, after the sun had set and a brief shower settled the dust, the fairgrounds took on a gloomy, deserted atmosphere. Fence boards became sinister—gray, red, then black as the sky paled, bled, and died. The general public had long since fled. Even the squirrels headed urgently to their nests, but not before that one last bite of discarded popcorn and a lap from the odd puddle of sweet spilled pop.

Only the rodeo performers were left behind. Of course Buck had the longest trailer in the lot, and too wide to slip easily into a normal parking space. It had his name emblazoned in gigantic letters on both sides. He'd hung bull horns above the door, which had a saddle horn for a knob and a horseshoe for a knocker, which he made himself.

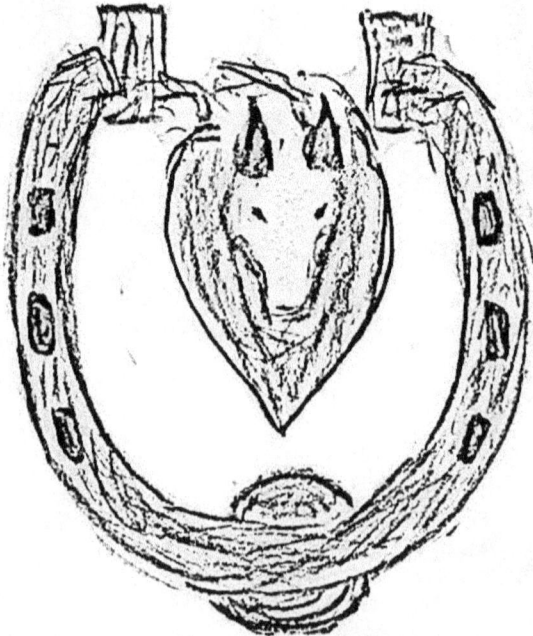

Buck could often be seen in his spare bedroom cleaning and polishing a hand gun. Mounted on the wall behind him was an imposing collection of pistols: Colts, Glocks, Remingtons, Brownings, Mausers, Smith and Wessons; the list was endless and disturbing. They were solid and powerful in his hands. They endowed him with these qualities, to the envy of all, he mused. Whenever a girl would hold one he'd carve a notch in it. It was Buck's dream to someday turn the rodeo into a true Wild West show—with real Indians and bullets. Blanks of course. Never mind that many of the guns were not old west revolvers but modern automatic magazine types. How bizarre would that be? Cowboys shooting Indians with Berettas. There were too many guns for the wall so he had his favorites spread out on the bed where he could hold and fondle them. He polished them often as he could. Naked steel, they looked so cold lying there on the sheet, but he knew how hot they could become in his hands. He fingered their triggers. His mouth watered. Before he went to bed he'd tuck them in with a soft blanket to keep out the dust. He loved them; they were precious to him. They sent exciting currents down his spine and shot tingles into girls.

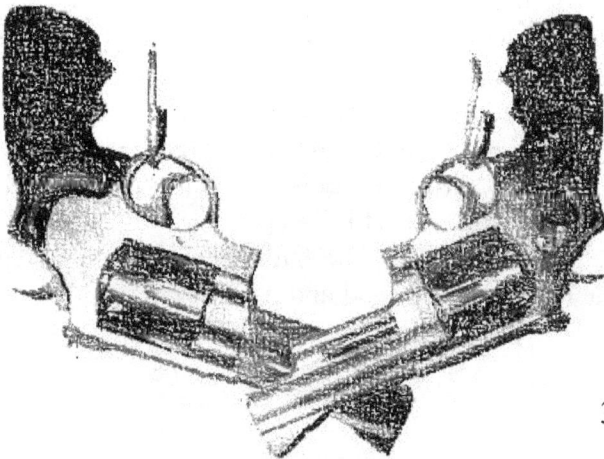

But not Curlygirl. She wandered aimlessly outside as the other females partied behind dimly lit windows. She kicked a stone and it hit a gate, disturbing a few nearby horses. An owl flew over ominously and a cat crept behind a wall. The place smelled like stale hay and it seemed like an evil dankness was setting in. Slowly a fog began devouring the definitions of trees and trails. After a brief but hard shower the girl was wet as an otter's pocket. A cold impulse shot down her back so she headed to the horse barn. Her legs felt weak and her face was marked with dust-caked tears. Her mouth was dry. She just wanted to hug something—even a horse would do.

When she got back to her stall, there was Ponyboy standing by her mare in the dim light, wearing a dim-witted grin. He was hunched over in his usual timid manner. Astonished, she walked right up to his face. She was surprised that her shyness seemed to wane when she was around this boy.

"What are you doing with my horse?" she demanded—a little more forcefully than she intended..

He knew what he wanted to reply but just gazed stupidly at her dirty boots. Finally he said, "I... I just wanted to know why you would wear such a crucifix." That was not on his mind at all, but that's what came out of his mouth.

She grabbed it protectively. "He's my man, I told you. He died for me. See, right here on this cross. I wouldn't expect you to know anything about that. Just forget it."

"But I do know," he said, becoming more erect. "He rose from the dead and paid for all our sins."

"Maybe you're a sinner," she said, "but I've been good all my life."

He nervously fingered a few strands of horse mane. "*Romans 3:23* says all have sinned and fall short of the glory of God."

"Of course I'm not good as God," she replied, "but the Bible says I'm a Princess of Christ. Right fella? And that's good enough for me. And who cares what those old Romans said anyway! They were nasty people who slept naked then wore their bed sheets around in the day."

Ponyboy cocked his head, then shrugged his shoulders. "Of course you're a princess," he said finally (she certainly looked and acted like one), "so would you like to come to a Bible study with me?"

"No."

His shoulders slumped and he turned to leave. "There are many theories about arguin' with a woman," he thought to himself. "—None of them work."

Then Curlygirl saw that he had absentmindedly left his big number 12 pinned to his back. Her eyes followed it out of the building. "Yes, okay." She said it too softly to be heard but her words followed him like ghosts. Ponyboy stopped in his tracks.

"Seven PM Wednesday," he mumbled and continued on his way. He must be completely out of his mind, he thought. But she heard.

A few days passed like alley-cats on a wall. It was soon 6:30 and Ponyboy was at Curlygirl's door. He braced himself and was careful to jump off the steps after knocking. She was there instantly, wearing that crucifix, a suede purse, and her leather-bound Bible. Her bouncy, curly hair dazzled his eyes. He raised a hand to help her down the steps but she waved it off—and their fingers brushed briefly. By accident on purpose, they each reflected. The meandering stroll over to the rec room would be sheer delight. He would be proud to be seen with her, his arm at the small of her back. Their fingers would almost touch several times again and neither would be surprised by the electricity involved. It was the kind of current that travels through air.

Suddenly as they rounded the corner of a building there was Buck, smack-dab in Ponyboy's face and grabbing the front of his shirt. It looked like he had a gun in his pants.

"Leave my girl alone," he growled, "or I'll give you a black eye and a red nose." His massive arms lifted Ponyboy clear off the ground and smashed him into the wall. Buck's biceps bulged like footballs. Everything on him bulged. Everything on Ponyboy was limp.

Curlygirl tried to thrust herself between them in protest, but by then Buck had the boy by the throat. "Stop it, Buck," she cried, but the big cowboy just squeezed harder and harder. Ponyboy was beginning to choke and drool. He was turning purple. The girl became desperate. Finally she stammered, "Okay, okay. You can have it." She stood on her tiptoes and gave the big brute a big wet kiss on the cheek. His cheek was sweaty and the stubble was prickly to her lips. He smelled of beer. But his neck muscles started to relax. Finally he dropped Ponyboy in the dust and turned to embrace the small girl hanging on his arm. Men are so hardwired, she thought to herself. They're all knobs and stick shifts; you can control them like lawn tractors—John Deeres who deserve Dear Johns.

Just then a group of cowboys happened by so Curlygirl grabbed the fallen boy and the two hobbled off. There was more meandering to catch their breaths and brush off dust but eventually they arrived at the Bible study in one piece. Standing faithfully outside was the clown's old white horse. His name was Faithful. True to his name, he never had to be tied up. You always knew where the clown was because of old Faithful.

Ponyboy held the door for Curlygirl. He was glad that she would enter first, to field the questions since they were new, and because he was somewhat disheveled. Yet once inside she scampered to an empty chair between two girls—leaving Ponyboy to awkwardly sit next to the clown himself and a greasy-trousered man he didn't know from Adam. How unfaithful of her. There were three men and five women now in the circle. Ponyboy was surprised that there were so many at a Bible study. Yet few if any, he assumed would be true Christians like himself.

The clown looked quite ordinary without his baggy pants and painted grin. Normal and unassuming even. Yet he did have one humongous secret, but figured that "lettin' the cat outta the bag is a whole lot easier than puttin' it back in." He was quiet, slender, balding and had a thin, slightly misshapen nose (still a bit red) and a crooked little smile. He was not old, but looked it. Maybe that was why he never married.

He'd already been talking so he just said, "Welcome guys," and didn't embarrass the newcomers further. "As we were seeing," he continued in a pleasant resonating voice, "in *Matthew 5:3* we find the first Beatitude. These are statements of happiness made by Jesus in the Sermon on the Mount. Their basic message is that born-again people are blessed with certain internal qualities and external features. Just think of it! They are not things to strive for. They are not sayings to make us feel guilty because we don't have them. They are not things we'll get if we work hard at being better people. They are not even meant to motivate us. They are simply things God gives us through His grace when we give Him our lives. And they are all free gifts that we don't even deserve."

Curlygirl noticed that Ponyboy had found the passage instantly. His Bible was in such bad shape as to be almost desecrated and sacrilegious. For his part he noticed that her pages were lily white and untouched—much like herself. Curlygirl couldn't believe that she had just kissed Buck. But she did it to save Ponyboy. To protect him from Buck, maybe she had better find someone else to be sweet on. You can't have a relationship with a dead body. Her thoughts were wandering.

She had difficulty finding the passage so had to be helped by the girl next to her. Suddenly Ponyboy recognized this girl as the Native who rode beside Curlygirl in the parades. This girl had the beautiful chestnut mare with white socks—much like her rider. Well if this Native was a Christian she was certainly keeping it well hidden, Ponyboy reflected.

The Native seemed very spirited and her lustrous long, straight black hair commanded the room like a queen. Her smile, whenever she let it out was the brightest thing at the rodeo. Still everyone knew her secret. Several years ago Buck had coerced her to tattoo his initials on her tummy. It was her coming-of-age birthmark but she now wore it as the scar of an old nature she couldn't quite shake off. Buck thought of it as a notch on one of his pistols. So she did her best to keep it concealed. Even in summer that wasn't hard. Now that she was born-again, her smile was the birth-mark of a new nature in Christ. She glanced over at Ponyboy who was inspecting cracks in the floor and wondered why he would be at a Bible study anyway. If he was a Christian he was certainly keeping it well hidden.

Suddenly her hand shot up like an excited school girl.

"Jaycee Williams," called the clown.

Ponyboy's jaw dropped a little. He had thought that "Jaycee Williams" was the new cowboy riding bucking broncos. This one was a lot better looking. He gazed at her and started to experience some cowboy cravings. His eyes began grazing and glazing. Curlygirl notices such things and a cynical smile crossed her face, but she kept her nose well down into her Bible so as not to be called upon.

"Why does God leave evil Satan here on this earth?" Jaycee asked.

The question was off topic and the clown was a little disappointed that nobody seemed particularly moved by his description of the Beatitudes. He had worked on it a long time. How marvelous are the gifts that God gives to His people! Yet they seem mesmerized by everyday cares and pleasures. Eyes appear to wander and thoughts drift to earthly pursuits.

Nevertheless, he answered Jaycee with a smile. "For this we can go all the way back to Satan's role in Genesis 3. He was there to tempt man to sin. The snake offered Eve a lie that the fruit God had forbidden would not kill them, but make them wise. Eve liked that and enticed her husband. So Adam, the Father patriarch of all mankind, also made the choice to reject God—and that act was in effect a device of mass destruction, resulting in wholesale separation from God, a curse over all creation, past, present and future which propagates through the male line even today. Why is Satan still here? Why that God might be glorified! God is glorified and we are purified when we deny Satan and choose Christ as more desirable than our sinful cravings."

Ponyboy looked quickly away from Jaycee but her image remained on his retina and branded deeper within as a sinful craving. But how do you blot out beauty from your mind? Beauty attaches to the soul and blends with it. Beauty folds in and gratifies. He hardly noticed that she was talking again.

"But why isn't Jesus here now to help us against Satan?" Jaycee asked.

"Here's an illustration," said the clown. "Suppose God was the owner of a rodeo and He wanted everyone in it to grow and mature into fine, moral men and women. Make right choices. Live upright lives pleasing to him. Then the rodeo itself would be a witness that people who truly choose God lead worthwhile lives. They aren't necessarily wealthy, but rich in the things that matter. This would make God attractive to the general public, don't you think? It would give him glory. It would be better than God using smother-love to push people around like clay toys."

"Still, I wish he were closer somehow," Jaycee said.

"Well, he is," said the clown, "closer than you think. He owns the entire Rodeo and he will again return and take charge. Meanwhile he has sent his Holy Spirit as a helper and you have many opportunities to make right choices."

Jaycee smiled at Ponyboy but didn't say anything. He was her choice.

"Jesus has chosen me," piped up Curlygirl, "and I choose him. I love him. We are in love."

"I'm so glad to hear that," said the clown, "Now as to the Beatitudes, what do you think the first one means?"

Jaycee waved her hand but the clown called on Curlygirl, startling her. There was an awkward pause while she cleared her mind of Ponyboy and Buck sword fighting. "I think we should give money to the poor," she said.

Ponyboy immediately read the passage from his NIV. "'*Matthew 5:³Blessed are the poor in spirit, for theirs is the kingdom of heaven.*' **In spirit**." He was about to say something more but Jaycee broke in.

"Which means that God's kingdom is made up of the forgiven."

"And we should stop sinning," added Ponyboy.

Jaycee sent him the kind of smile that Curlygirl didn't appreciate, but he certainly did.

"This is all true," said the clown, "but we're missing one important point. God blesses those who *realize* their need for him. This is implied information. Perhaps I would interpret it like this:

"Verse 3. O how God blesses those who realize their helplessness and trust Him for the perfect obedience that shows they are part of His Kingdom."

"Jesus blesses me every day with his love," said Curlygirl. She was starting to relax and had the sweetest expression on her candy face.

"Yes he does," said the clown with a smile. "Now the second Beatitude reads like this: '⁴*Blessed are those who mourn, for they shall be comforted.*' What does it mean to mourn?"

"To feel sorry for yourself!" blurted Jaycee without raising her hand.

"Not only for yourself," said the clown, "but sorry for the whole worldwide rebellion against

God which causes the earth's suffering. You know, most people on earth are riding false religions straight into hell, others fashion gods in their own image and worship them as idols. Still others deny the concept of god altogether and in doing so set themselves up as their own god. What arrogance! And how bitter in the mouth of the real God who made them, loves the unlovable. He sent his son to take on their just punishment, thereby offering them forgiveness and life with him for all eternity. But still he is rejected. People choose hell by wishing it away. This is what I mourn for, not for the price of gas or the fat content of a hamburger. So, blessed are those who mourn. How does this sound for the second Beatitude?

"Verse 4. O how God blesses those whose hearts are broken by their own sin and by the world's rebellion and suffering, for amidst such sorrow God gives them supreme joy."

Curlygirl wondered silently if this kind of joy wouldn't be even better than a big hug from her fantasy prince Jesus. Jaycee wondered if this kind of joy would be able to erase the scars of her past and bitter heritage. Ponyboy felt sorry for all the miserable lives around him because they lacked his true belief.

The clown continued with the third Beatitude. "The ESV says: *⁵Blessed are the meek, for they shall inherit the earth.'* Who are the meek?"

Ponyboy loved this verse because he could identify with it so well. "Meek is not being angry or aggressive," he said, "not making waves, keeping to yourself, never missing a chance to keep your trap shut."

"I'm known for speaking my mind," said Jaycee giving him a playful look, "is that so wrong?"

"When you're a blabbermouth, it is," said Curlygirl almost under her breath. "Just kidding," she added softly. But the battle lines had been drawn.

Jaycee returned an icy stare, "Shut it, little titmouse. Oh sorry, sorry," she added with her mouth turned down and her nose turned up.

With flashes of eye anger they both looked over at Ponyboy for some indication as to who had won the skirmish. But the boy only pulled his head in like a turtle and said nothing. Should he choose striking beauty or irresistible cuteness? But this was shocking behavior at a Bible study. So immature. Still the attention was stimulating, but it was twisting his guts. Maybe it was mostly in his mind. Nevertheless he stared pleadingly at the clown who continued hastily with the lesson.

"Well then here's how I'd put it:

"Verse 5. O how God blesses the girl who is always angry at the proper time and never angry improperly. Who keeps her emotions under control because she herself is God-controlled. She is humble to realize her own ignorance and weakness. Such a girl is like a queen of all the earth."

Both Jaycee and Curlygirl liked the idea of being a queen, but they both knew that there could be only one queen in the castle. So they steeled themselves for the inevitable fight to the death.

Almost everybody having missed the main points presented, the rest of the Bible study was devoted to prayer and cupcakes. Ponyboy had three and prayed that more "skin" Christians would become truly born-again like himself. Jaycee prayed that God would show her when to be angry and when to be sweet. At Curlygirl's turn she prayed very softly that she would learn to love the Lord as much as He loved her. Secretly she just wanted to smash her cupcake into Jaycees big fake smile. The clown wondered silently if having a Bible study for this crowd was useless as setting a milk bucket under a bull.

"Next week we'll tackle the next 3 Beatitudes," he said. It was awkward as they all stood up to leave and shuffled like cattle toward the door. Curlygirl noticed that Jaycee was cutting Ponyboy out like a calf. The Indian nudged him with her big hips and drove him outside, away from the other girls. The two disappeared down a path together, giggling and grinning like monkeys. Curlygirl was headed in the same direction so she followed at a distance fuming. It looked like their hands were almost touching. Was that his arm around her in the fog? Or was she just incredibly fat? It looked like that could have been a kiss at her door. Curlygirl expected him to go inside but instead he hopped over to his trailer and popped in. Was he dancing? He was acting like a young colt. Why didn't he fall off *Jaycee's* steps? Their trailers were right next to each other. She couldn't decide which one to set on fire first, so she just turned towards home in tears.

Chapter 4
The Stump Race

It was another day, another town—same old rodeo. Jaycee had again managed to park her rig right next to Ponyboy's. But even closer this time. Adjoining windows, thought Curlygirl as she drove up. She could see them in his kitchen already frying dinner. He was calling her Jay now and she was referring to themselves as "PB & J." They were jumping from the frying pan into the fire. Enough to make you hurl. Curlygirl just pulled through and parked all the way over by the horse stables. Buck's trailer was right in the middle and as usual there was a Wild West party going on in it. In the living room was a lot of silly liquor play, pistols in the bedrooms, and vomiting everywhere else. Curlygirl just buried her head in her pillow to shut out the noise—and the world.

The next morning she was leaning on the fence watching Buck and Ponyboy duke it out in the points standings. Beside her was Faithful keeping watch over his beloved master, called Truth. Ponyboy was in the arena trying to keep a bucking bronco between him and the ground and the clown was trying his best to keep the landing as soft as possible.

"Who's gunna win?" It was Jaycee coming up behind her and pressing in way too close.

"I am, actually," said Curlygirl, thinking she was referring to their contest over the bronc rider.

"Oh I doubt that," came the reply, "I'm faster than you in everything."

"That's for sure," Curlygirl fluttered, "but not in rodeo events."

"Oh yes, especially those," said Jaycee, "sometimes I wish we could bet money on it."

"Hmmm," muttered Curlygirl, "how about betting Ponyboy on it; he's worth something, yuh think?" Human trafficking in men has not entirely died out in the American West.

Jaycee thought for a moment. "But I already have him."

"You may be dug in like a tick," said Curlygirl, "but not deep enough in his heart, and you know it. I could come in after what's mine anytime I want."

Jaycee hesitated. "Not if I beat you in the race today, okay little Miss Titmouse?"

Curlygirl's tiny knees trembled but she agreed. "Okay you're on, missy fancy pants. We're paired today. It's for Ponyboy then. Winner take all."

"It's a pleasure," said Jay, "see ya later." She slapped Curlygirl on the shoulder—a trifle too hard to be entirely friendly.

The event in question was a Camas Prairie Stump Race, first played by the Nez Perce Native American tribe. How ironic thought Curlygirl to be paired with a Native today. The very one who thought she could steal her boy away. It's actually a barrel race in which two horses race each other on identical courses opposite the start-finish line. The riders start facing opposite directions and the first one back across wins.

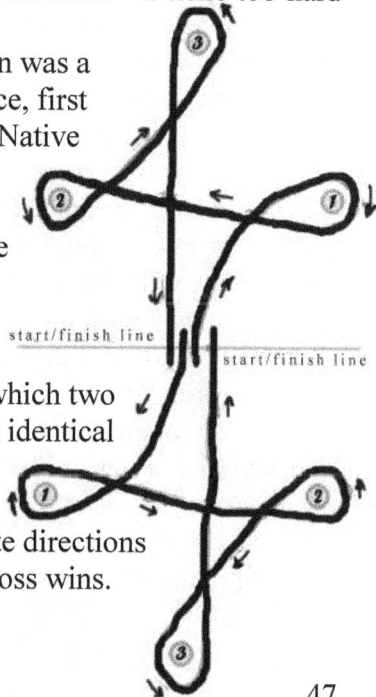

start/finish line

start/finish line

Now it was Ponyboy's turn to watch the cowgirls. Nonchalantly, he sat on the top rail of the fence. He only knew two of them well. Of the two Jay had the faster record, and clearly she was the most glamorous and friendly. The beauty. She was easy to look at and even easier to talk with. Her outfit had more sequins. After knowing her just a couple weeks she was already a lump of soft candy in his mouth. Miss Jaycee Williams.

Still, Curlygirl was the cutest thing since Tinker Bell and everything about her was nymph-like and sprightly. Her shape was delicate. Her hair bouncy. But she was rather short for him and short *with* him at times too. Plus, she had peculiar ideas about Jesus—like He was her boyfriend or something. So, when all was said and done Jay might be the better catch. But Curlygirl was—well in spite of everything, could it be possible he was still in love with this pixie? How to choose? Would God decide such a thing? Come to think about it, of course he would. God is sovereign and determines everything, right? Ponyboy decided to talk to the clown about it before the next Bible study.

The race interrupted his thoughts and his two sweethearts were paired and ready. Neither could possibly win the overall prize but this race would be even more interesting. Girlfriends at odds. Would it be too wicked to watch? Maybe he should take the winner—never mind any spiritual qualifications. It looked to him like they were really getting into the spirit of competition.

Facing opposite, Curlygirl nudged her horse into Jay's leg much the same way that Buck tried to push her around. Jay retaliated and soon there was a bit of a shoving match going on. There was a lot of sparring, bumping, leaning & pulling. Their eyes locked on to each other and eventually Jay leaned over and grabbed Curlygirl's sleeve in an attempt to pull her off her horse. But Curlygirl grabbed on and spurred her mount, unseating Jay and spilling her into the dust. The crowd in the stands gasped at such behavior, but then started clapping, thinking it to be part of the show. Soon their boots were pounding as fast as their hearts.

Jay was mad as a slapped hornet but couldn't catch Curlygirl who was still on horseback and kicking up dust. Eventually just as Jay had remounted and positioned herself again at the start line the horn sounded and they were off like bunnies in opposite directions. Around the barrels they sped with such reckless abandon that Ponyboy was sure one of them would end up eating dirt. They were actually yelling at their horses as if the rest of their lives depended on it. He had never seen such hysteria. On the turns the hooves dug deep into the ground and on the straightaways the riders clung fast to the horses' manes. Their whole bodies became one bounding and furious horse motion. It was over in sixteen seconds.

Jay was clearly the winner but just after dashing across the finish line she veered aside and with a war cry, rammed Curlygirl head-on off her course in a collision which tumbled the smaller girl to the ground. It must have been the first time since Indian days that someone failed to finish. Humiliated, Curlygirl skedaddled directly out the gate and off to her trailer. Jay pranced about on her war horse but soon was not quite so proud of herself. Eventually she too made a hasty retreat.

After the dust had settled, Ponyboy on a whim bounded over the railing and trotted across to retrieve Curlygirl's mare which was standing timidly over against a far fence. He led her solemnly to a stall in the big barn and brushed her down nicely.

Did God determine the outcome of this race? It was way early for the Bible study but Ponyboy found himself standing beside Faithful and knocking at Truth's door to pose just that question.

"God is completely in charge, so would he determine the outcome of a silly barrel race, for instance?" Ponyboy asked, once they were settled.

"God determines everything," said the clown, "even what we have for dinner, when we sneeze and who we marry. He counts the hairs on our heads and names each star."

Ponyboy jumped on this immediately. "Yeah, but what about my freewill to choose whatever girl I may want? God has already chosen that, I suppose?"

"Let me try to explain," said the clown. "It seems like God's predestination and our freewill are not compatible concepts; either God chooses or you choose, right? But it's possible to understand both as being true without being logically inconsistent. God is absolutely sovereign, knows and controls all. Yet man, in His image, is called to make genuine decisions: 1. to place his faith in Christ for salvation, 2. to decide for himself what he wants to do, and 3. to pray, which may influence the outcome of events. These two positions may seem contradictory, but in the mind of God they make perfect sense. *'1 Corinthians 13:12. For now we see in a mirror dimly, but then face to face.'*

"Omniscient God, who knows and controls past, present, and future all in the same instant from a vantage point outside of time and space, created men, who are free to make choices in the present that have ramifications in the future. So both are true. I call this **bilateralism**. God is absolutely sovereign and therefore controls any choice that a human can make, he is even the author of our very faith in him. Yet at the same time God is right to hold humans accountable because from their perspective within the confines of serial time, humans make real moral choices between good and evil."

Speaking about time, Ponyboy checked his watch for his life of late was being governed by it. Eight seconds here, seven seconds there, sixteen, and now 7 PM. He didn't want to be late.

Chapter 5
Holding Hands

Captivating as discussing God in the clown's trailer was, Ponyboy noticed that it was almost time for Bible study so he ducked out quickly to pick up Jay. She was his new flame and he was her devoted moth. Curlygirl might be his one true love but she had treated him like a dog chewing a wasp. Truly, he found Jaycee fascinating and now finishing up the dishes in his kitchen. Was his life going down the drain? As he entered, her eyes ate him up like a hound on hamburger. Soon she was tickling and snapping the dishtowel at him. They touched hands, hips, noses and strolled arm-in-arm back to the clown's place.

"Say," she asked as they got close to the door, "have you ever wondered if a clown is the right sort of person to lead a Bible study?"

"He sure seems to know a lot," said Ponyboy, giving her a sideways glance and then a squeeze around the waist. "And he saves cowboys every day. Clowns can be misunderstood."

"But I mean he's not a pastor or a priest or anything official," Jaycee said. "Also he sure does tend to get wound-up when preaching at us."

"I don't think that a separate clergy class is a biblical concept," replied Ponyboy. "He's okay in my book so long as he's spinning out good Bible teaching. Being wound-up is fine with me if it's the Holy Spirit that does the winding." He gave her another side hug, but harder. He could feel her ribs. Soon they were at the door and he was trying to playfully count them before entering. Old Faithful snorted at him as if in disapproval. Would a horse care about such things?

"No, I mean how do we know he's authorized for this?" she asked, trying halfheartedly to push him away.

Just at that time Curlygirl arrived and timidly nudged them aside to get to the door. "Thanks for bringing my horse home," she muttered to Ponyboy and gave Jaycee a condescending look straight into her omnipresent teeth.

Ponyboy reached to open the door for the tiny cowgirl but Jay pulled him away by the waist. So Curlygirl went in by herself, followed by the couple, and then a few others. When all were seated the clown greeted everyone and began.

Or rather Jaycee began with a question.

"Since we always do shows on Sunday, and never get to church in the summer—well how come we never get communion, and is that a bad thing?"

The clown answered immediately. "Communion was instituted by our Lord at the Last Supper. The Bible says in *Matthew 26:26, 'Now as they were eating, Jesus took bread, and after blessing it broke it and gave it to the disciples, and said, "Take, eat; this is my body."'* Yes Jaycee it's a bad thing not to obey that commandment. Would you all like to do it now?"

Curlygirl seemed hesitant, Ponyboy reluctant, but Jaycee dashed immediately over to the kitchen area and returned with a dry dinner roll and a two liter coke. "Will this do?" she asked.

The clown took the bun, broke off a piece and passed the rest around. "Thank you Lord for sacrificing your body on the cross for our sins." They took a moment to reflect silently on how they had offended God, then they all ate.

The clown continued, "The next two verses say, *'And he took a cup, and when he had given thanks he gave it to them, saying, "Drink of it, all of you, for this is my blood of the covenant, which is poured out for many for the forgiveness of sins."'*

"This coke," the clown continued, "being the only 'wine' we have, we will use it, and may the Lord bless it." They passed around the plastic bottle and all sipped from it. That may seem unsanitary but cowboys have their own standards.

"Was that really a communion?" asked Curlygirl.

"Was it reverent and relevant?" the clown asked rhetorically. There was silence. "Well I have something else for you then. In *John 6:35* Jesus says, *'I am the bread of life; whoever comes to me shall not hunger, and whoever believes in me shall never thirst.'* Thus Jesus provides for our eating and drinking, but also this is a picture of his salvation and care for his people. Consider his miracles. First in *John 2* he provided wine for a wedding. The six large stone jugs were for Jewish purification rites. However when Jesus turned the water into wine, it was a picture of how his blood would purify those who believe in him.

"Later at Bethsaida he fed five loaves of bread and two fish to 5,000 men in *Luke 9:10-17*. Bethsaida was a Jewish town in Galilee, Peter's hometown. When all had eaten they collected twelve baskets of leftovers.

"He also fed 4000 men under similar circumstances in Decapolis, an area predominately Gentile (not Jewish). *Mark 7:31; 8:1-10*. Here there were seven baskets of leftovers."

"So how come we have these two stories in the Bible with the same meaning?" Jaycee asked.

"What's the meaning?" the clown asked back.

"Well that God will supply all our needs," Jaycee replied, "and also that we shouldn't be wasteful with food or litter the environment. Same meaning for both."

"Okay, yes," said the clown, "but let's dig a little deeper. This is an example of how it's possible infer a deeper understanding of God directly from the Scriptures.

"Jesus fed 5,000 Jews and afterwards they collected twelve baskets of leftovers. The number twelve often symbolizes the nation of Israel. Remember the twelve tribes of Israel? So Jesus is the bread of life for Israel.

"Now look at this. Later Jesus fed 4000 Gentiles and afterwards they collected seven baskets of leftovers. The number seven denotes completeness and perfection. So Jesus is showing that he will add non-Jews like us into his kingdom. *Acts 1:8* says, *'But you will receive power when the Holy Spirit has come upon you, and you will be my witnesses in Jerusalem and in all Judea and Samaria, and to the end of the earth.'*

"So all these rich ideas," said the clown, "stem directly from our simple act of eating from a bun and sipping Coke."

At this point Jaycee said something amazing. "Hey, I think I get it. You're just tying up bits of the Bible to make up a single idea—the way we harness horses into a team for more power. For instance, Moses' first public miracle of changing water, the Nile river, into blood. This would tie Moses as the first savior of his Jews through their escape from Egypt to Jesus later as the spiritual savior of his church."

"I'm so glad I can be a part of that church," said Curlygirl and everyone agreed in their hearts.

There was silence as the special moment soon passed. The clown looked down into his Bible. "We are in *Matthew 5*, *"⁶Blessed are those who hunger and thirst for righteousness, for they shall be satisfied."*"

Curlygirl noticed how easily Jaycee and Ponyboy found the passage since they were using but one Bible. "And they may as well have been using but one chair," she thought. "And holding hands during a Bible study? Shouldn't that be sacrilegious, ya think?" She knew what Jaycee was really hungering and thirsting for. Maybe she could say amazing things about the Bible but that girl was full of herself and causing her Ponyboy to stumble into sin.

The clown chimed into these thoughts with his paraphrase of the verse they were looking at.

"6. O how God blesses the person who aches to be morally good as much as a starving man hankers for food, or a girl in the desert yearns for water—for that person is totally fulfilled in Christ!"

It was hilarious to watch. At these words the joined hands, like naughty children slowly and silently uncoupled and slunk away into their own respective laps. Then Curlygirl perceived some daylight between hips, shoulders no longer touching, and even the use of separate Bibles. "The hoe has been busted on God's solid ground," she thought, "God punishes slinky girls who try to slip man-hearts away from their rightful owners."

But again the clown crept into her head with the next verse.

"⁷Blessed are the merciful, for they shall receive mercy.

"7. O how God blesses the girl who gets right inside other people's minds so she can see with their eyes, think with their thoughts, feel with their feelings and reason with their reasons. This girl will find compassion and others will do the same for her. She will know that this is what Jesus has done as well."

Curlygirl admitted to herself that Jaycee might have pure intentions toward Ponyboy after all, but if they were anything like her own, they were not all lily white. Almost every flower has its roots in dirt. Compassion for others? Compassion in a stump race is like a donkey in a derby. Or was it a jousting match? She had ended up on the ground anyway. Ponyboy had been the jackass lately. At least Buck was steadfast in his pursuit of her. At least he was being a man—all man, pure hard muscleman and making her feel desirable as pure silk draped over him. She always knew where she stood with him.

Ponyboy for his part examined his motives toward Jaycee. Clearly he was letting his fallen nature rope him like a calf. He was falling prey to the warmth of a smile and the heat of a moment. His cowboy cravings, he decided were completely self-serving and without compassion for Jaycee. He prayed furtively that his thoughts and actions would become more pure.

Jaycee, on the other hand didn't mind a little stallion blood in a man so long as she could ride it hard and rein it in whenever necessary. With Ponyboy she needed spurs more often than reins however but the result was pure horseplay—a

57

proper prancing performance. She didn't see anything so immoral or impure about galloping, cantering, or even daydreaming about an especially bouncy trot someday. After all, weren't horses and riders created for all that?

"*8Blessed are the pure in heart, for they shall see God.*" The clown was again having his way of intruding into thoughts and the Bible its way of messing with messed up minds.

"8. O the delight of the person whose motives are absolutely pure, for that person sees God."

Like little Adam and Eves most of the people around the circle started to hang their heads, not wanting to be seen by God, or Truth for that matter. At least they were catching the meaning now and starting to weave mental fig leaves around the private parts of their brains. But nothing fundamental seemed to be changing. After some prayer, platitudes and pastry there was a somber exit from the Bible study. Curlygirl looked especially subdued on her way out so the clown slipped something into her hand.

"Why are you hiding from me, Curlygirl?" he asked.

"My thoughts seemed naked in front of all these people," she said, "so I hid them. I didn't feel safe. What's this paper"?

"It's my humble interpretation of the Armor of God. You may need it tonight, I perceive," he said.

Curlygirl thought of just stuffing it into her pocket, but then sat down to skim it over—so as not to hurt his feelings. She is a girl who always wants to please, she reflected. The first part was typed. A few key words jumped out at her boldly.

"Ephesians 6:¹³ Therefore take up the whole **armor of God***, that you may be able to withstand in the* **evil day***, and having done all, to stand firm.* *¹⁴ Stand therefore, having fastened on the* **belt of truth***, and having put on the* **breastplate of righteousness***, ¹⁵ and, as* **shoes** *for your feet, having put on the readiness given by the* **gospel of peace***.* *¹⁶ In all circumstances take up the* **shield of faith***, with which you can extinguish all the flaming darts of the evil one; ¹⁷ and take the* **helmet of salvation***, and* **the sword of the Spirit***, which is the* **word** *of God,"*

The clown continued in his own handwriting.

"Belt of TRUTH – Jesus is the only way for me, the only truth that's real, and the only life worth living. I will flee from other gods of my own making. I will study God's sovereignty, holiness, wisdom, and love.

"Breastplate of RIGHTEOUSNESS – I will believe in Jesus Christ and his death on the cross, which frees me from slavery to my sin nature and self-indulgent habits. I will recognize and reject the evil ways of this world.

"Shoes of PEACE – I will dwell with inner joy in my eternal union with Jesus Christ, and resist demonic spirits and practices. Peace is not the absence of trouble but the presence of Christ.

"Shield of FAITH – I will continually trust in God, and the promises of His Word. I will reject commands from inner wisdom, dreams, visions, spirits, voices, forces, coincidences, and indeed anything which does not elevate God.

"Helmet of SALVATION – I will focus on God's promises of daily and eternal rescue in Jesus. I will grow in Him only. I do not evolve spiritually by increasing in consciousness through connection to any power but Christ.

"Sword of the Spirit, His WORD – I will use the power of God's Word to defeat deception and triumph over my spiritual enemies. I will flee the power of any other thoughts, pronouncements, or incantations to direct spiritual forces or manipulate reality.

"And for the strength to do all this I will rely solely on the power of my Lord Jesus Christ by responding to his indwelling Holy Spirit in obedience."

When Curlygirl looked up she was alone with the clown. "Thanks for this," she said, "I'll use it this very night."

"How so?" asked the clown.

"Well, I was trying to decide whether to go to Buck's party," said the girl, "but if I wear this armor I can go for sure. Maybe I'll even be able to witness there."

"Young lady," it was as if the clown was addressing a teenager, "it won't help. If you go somewhere you shouldn't, then you're disobeying God and taking off the armor—especially the breastplate of righteousness. I wouldn't enter into the evil ways of this world. You won't be safe."

"But I can do all things thorough Christ who strengthens me. I'm his princess. He loves me." With this she rushed out the door, leaving the clown's reply falling to the floor at her heals. Once outside, her thoughts turned immediately to Buck and his godlike stature. She loved Jesus but Buck was "the rest of" her Jesus. The part that made her tingle and the part she could see and feel. Feel enchanted and protected by. Well maybe tonight she would see. Would it be a sin to follow natural, God-given feelings?

Chapter 6
On the Brink

Curlygirl hurried back to her trailer and yanked on shorts and a tank top. Shaking out her hair was enough and she didn't need makeup. Makeup was sinful to her. On the way to Buck's she noticed both Ponyboy's and Jaycee's trailers were dark. Which one would they be in and why dark? Which sinners are worse, evil doers or those who only imagine? Such questions were torture, so she hurried along and burst into Buck's place like a bird into a cage of circus cats. She fluttered about and soon found he was sitting on the sofa with another girl. In spite of this she alighted at his other side, almost spilling their drinks. The tall girl gave her an icy expression and grasped at him with cheetah-like arms.

"Juicy Fruit!" Buck exclaimed. "Howdy to yah and how are yah? Here, let me get you a drink." He got up so fast the two girls almost fell upon each other. And would have, had it not been for the drink that one held. The tall girl had big black eyes, a pointy nose, and a tiny red-lipped mouth. Her small head swiveled on a long, slender neck. She continued her penetrating stare as if projecting a laser dot on Curlygirl's forehead.

"I'll have a coke," Curlygirl chirped to Buck's broad back. She turned her head to avoid the tall girl's gaze.

Buck spun around wide-eyed, "Cokes are bad fer yah figure," but came back straight away with a bottle. He seemed to have everything. Curlygirl found that a bottle in her mouth protected her from having to say much. Besides, her curly blond hair and big bashful eyes did most of the talking. Finally the tall girl got tired of hanging on Buck's back and bounded off out the door.

Curlygirl noticed that everyone there was part of a lovebird pair. "Sapsuckers all," she reflected. Maybe this wasn't such a good idea after all. Would now be a good time to start witnessing about Jesus?

Buck brought her another coke; they were the small bottles. "I put rum in this one," he said. "Just kidding. But there *is* this." He produced a small white pill and popped it down the neck.

"What's *THAT*?" said the small girl, preparing to leave. In a trailer the door is never far away.

"Oh stop. It's only an aspirin. Helps you relax."

"Aspirin and coke is an aphrodisiac," said Curlygirl.

"That's a false urban legend," Buck said. He whipped out his cellphone and showed her proof from the internet. "Aspirin and caffeine is good for headaches. Won't make you high at all." Some of the other couples were agreeing, but one girl did seem strung out on something.

"Rope," said her fella, "she's at the end of her rope, haha—hard day on a horse." He laughed and carried her out the door like a saddle.

That seemed to be the signal for everyone to leave but Buck kept Curlygirl down on the couch with his pythonesque arm. For some reason she didn't fully mind and it was a buzz stroking the curves of such a large bicep. Soon she noticed that his shirt was off and the body underneath was shaped like a suit of armor. It bulged in all the right places like some great god's. Greek and glossy he was. Leathery. Hard and well oiled. It made her feel protected and relaxed. Being next to him was like riding her powerful horse, but now all the horses were flying. Among the clouds they were—blue here, grey there, charging and fighting, swift swords brandishing, terrible in their awe, and in their wake, woe. Pain. Screams. Confusion. Smoke. Shock. Civil War. Combat inside in her mind and yet she remained tranquil and limp. Then blessedly insensible.

The next morning she remembered nothing of Buck or anything that happened at the party. Did she even go to a party? What happened to the Armor of God? She remembered talking to the clown about it. Perhaps it didn't fit her properly. Can someone just rip it off? Later Truth told her she had probably been given Rohypnol, the so-called "date-rape drug." The symptoms he said are sedation, muscle relaxation, and a lowering of any apprehension. The drug causes strong amnesia so victims usually don't remember anything that happens. He offered to help her press charges but she declined because she was sure that nothing that awful had or could ever happen to her. The jealous God who loves her would have protected her. He held her in his hand. *Psalm 139:9-10*. She just knew it.

Meanwhile Ponyboy was burning up with fever for his truelove girl, a heat which no amount of Coca-Cola could cool. Dreaming about it only made it worse. Soon his work began to suffer. He'd much rather trot about with his girlfriend than gallop with his horse. Eventually one morning early he trudged out to the stables. In desperation he timidly approached Buck. "Sell me your diamond ring," he pleaded.

"Too rich for the likes of you!" laughed Buck. "And quite useless to you, I'm afraid."

"Never mind that, what's your price?" sputtered the smaller cowboy.

"More than you're worth, Poorboy," hissed Buck.

"More than this here horse of mine?" replied Ponyboy.

That stopped Buck in his tracks. Why that horse could win him all the calf roping and steer wrestling contests in the world. He would become the greatest cowboy of all time. His name would become legend—like "Wild Bill" Hickok or Hopalong Cassidy. People would sing his praises. Hundreds of cowgirls would faun all over him. Feel his whip and hat. Thousands would... Wait, he already had that. Okay, on top of that he could marry Curlygirl. He was always polite to her. Never mind the ring. With his winnings he could buy another. Why he could buy her ten, one for each finger.

Without even a thought about Ponyboy's wellbeing, or his feelings for his horse, Buck accepted the offer and began to roughly lead the bewildered animal away.

"Wait," Ponyboy called after him, "You haven't given me the ring yet."

"Consarn it, so I haven't," Buck remarked nonchalantly, reaching out his big hand, "here it is."

But Ponyboy still had an uneasy feeling. "One thing first," he said. "The deal doesn't close until midnight tomorrow. If I bring the ring back before then you'll return my horse."

Buck agreed and gave the horse a hard slap on the rump.

Curlygirl had awakened that morning knowing one thing: she hated men in general and wanted to strangle one in particular. But it wasn't Buck. Jaycee Williams on the other hand loved men in general and wanted to rustle up that very same one in particular. And lickety split.

She was having lunch with him in her trailer. It was his first time there since they always dated at his place. The days since last week's Bible study had given time for wise words to wear off and now the couple was like a pair of Roman Candles with fuses lit. Fittingly her trailer had a love seat so she pressed him into it, then offered something to drink before settling in beside.

"Are you thirsty?" she asked.

"Yes."

"Just a sec." She disappeared into a small bedroom. This gave Ponyboy opportunity to get nervous and to worry about the ring box making a bulge in his pants.

She jerked on shorts, a halter top and came out with fresh lipstick and newly combed hair. That made his legs feel funny so he stretched them out in front of him. There was an odd feeling in his stomach. She bent over a tiny refrigerator, popped two tall cans of beer, then bounced in hard up against his thigh. She deposited a cold one into his hand, then thrust frigid fingers under his shirt to make him squirm. That he did, spilling a bit of beer from both their cans. The alien smell of it filled his nostrils and he stiffened.

"What's wrong," she said, instinctively knowing the moods of a man.

"Well I'm just not that fond of beer, that's all."

"Why not?"

"No reason. I guess I'm just not used to it."

"Would you rather have wine?"

"No."

"Why?"

"Well ok, alcohol is sinful and sinful to drink."

"Really? Where do you get that? In the Bible?"

"It's the way I apply the Bible," he said defensively.

She frowned at him and her shoulders drooped. "I think moderate drinking is fine and teetotalers are misguided. They can be rude too by imposing their rigid ideas on others."

"They're safeguarding basic Biblical standards," he said.

"They're rude," she responded.

"You're being rude," he said.

She just stared at him, then grabbed his drink, got up, and poured it down the sink.

"Well, you could of drunk it," he said.

"I wouldn't want to sin so bad right in your face."

"You should pour yours out too then."

With that she took a long swig, then chugged most of the can before breathing. A tiny bit was running down her chin when she said, "I think I'll have another, if you don't mind."

"Well go ahead and knock yourself out," said Ponyboy. "Maybe I'll just slip out and not be in your way when you keel over."

"Maybe that's best," she said. "I wouldn't want to cause you to stumble."

"You're the one who's stumbling," he snapped and headed toward the door.

If you find yourself in a hole, the first thing to do is stop digging. So she did nothing to stop him but did wonder what that odd bulge in his pocket was. Hardly any of her concern she supposed, which turned out to be painfully true.

Chapter 7
The Truelove Girl

The next Bible study was not for three days. Everything had to fit around fluctuating rodeo schedules and travel days. Ponyboy, Curlygirl and Jaycee all came separately and sat as far away from each other as possible. Yet their eyes soon became engaged in a free-for-all wrestling match. Eventually Curlygirl's baby blues held her boy's momentarily but then he looked down into his Bible. Staring at girls was sinful to him. He was glad when the clown began.

But it was actually Jaycee who began by cutting him off in mid-sentence. "Oh please before we begin Truthful Sir, could you tell us what the Bible says about love, and about people who say they love you and then leave you over the smallest of lame excuses."

She eyed Ponyboy who felt provoked to add, "and also about people who wear skimpy clothes and drink too much beer." He didn't enjoy being prodded like a cow.

Curlygirl sat straight up and chimed in, "Why don't you two save part of your breath for breathin'!"

Now it was the clown's turn to squirm in his chair. "Well," he said, "I think the watchwords here are mindfulness, modesty and moderation. You know what I mean. You are big boys and girls. And you need to keep in mind the difference between love and lust. The Greek language of the Bible helps us here. *Eros* is lust, or sexual love like in marriage. It should be reserved for marriage. Yet there are three other words for love. **Storge** is 'affectionate love,' like for family or your spouse, **phileo** is 'brotherly love,' like for best friends, and **agape** is 'God-like, sacrificial, unconditional love.'"

Curlygirl piped up, "I love Jesus. Which love is that?"

Holding her off with his eyes, the clown continued, "*Matthew 22:36-39* reads:

"*³⁶'Teacher, which is the great commandment in the Law?' ³⁷ And he said to him, 'You shall love the Lord your God with all your heart and with all your soul and with all your mind. ³⁸ This is the great and first commandment. ³⁹ And a second is like it: You shall love your neighbor as yourself.'*"

"So the love in verse 37 must be **agape**, and **phileo** is in 39," said Ponyboy.

"Actually," said the clown, "they are both agape. We are to love our fellow man unconditionally, in a God-like manner. Agape has no selfish desires, gives indiscriminately without thought of return, and never diminishes or dies."

"Then what about brotherly love?" asked Jaycee. "I mean sisterly."

"An example of that would be in *1 Samuel 18* where *'the soul of Jonathan was knit to the soul of David, and Jonathan loved him as his own soul.'* We don't see a lot of that in our rodeo. Maybe 'trail hands' or partners in bullfighting would be examples. But Jesus is our greatest example of love because, *'Greater love has no one than this, that someone lay down his life for his friends.' John 15:13*.

"Did I ever tell you about my 'love triangles' theory? Love has three sides:

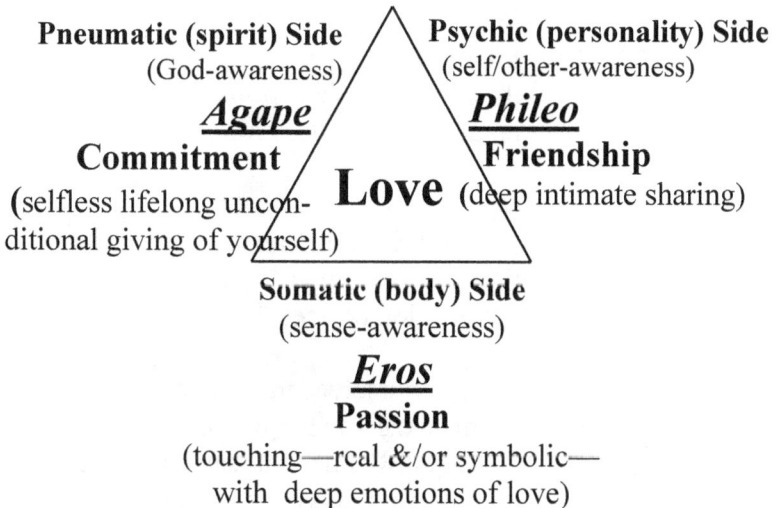

Pneumatic (spirit) Side   **Psychic (personality) Side**
(God-awareness)   (self/other-awareness)

Agape   *Phileo*

Commitment   **Friendship**
(selfless lifelong uncon- **Love** (deep intimate sharing)
ditional giving of yourself)

Somatic (body) Side
(sense-awareness)

Eros

Passion
(touching—real &/or symbolic—
with deep emotions of love)

71

"Good relationships start out small and grow in balance and in sync with the other person. So there are actually two triangles overlapping each other at every stage. One is hidden behind the other.

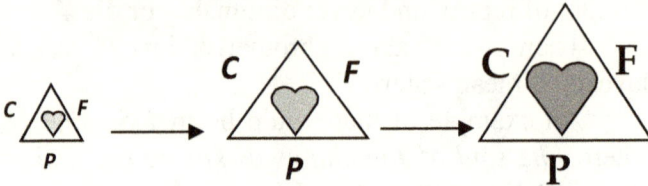

"Broken triangles mean false or shattered love—which only leads to pain.

When Friendship sharing exceeds the total of Commitment and Passion then over-familiarity breeds contempt.

When Commitment exceeds the total of Friendship and Passion then platonic obsession occurs resulting in fruitless infatuation.

When Passion is greater than the sum of Friendship and Commitment then the outcome is lustful prostitution of oneself.

"So can you see yourselves in these pictures? Can you see any mistakes you are making? Remember God is the only one who can 'fix' you. The key is to let him—and do your part. Being yoked with Christ is the only way that brings everlasting joy.

"One more thing about *agape,*" continued the clown, "since God is infinite in every respect he can't be divided. Infinity divided by any number is infinity. Therefore God adores each of his children with his whole attention and every bit of his love— as if each was the only person on earth."

"Jesus died for me," said Curlygirl. Jaycee knew that to be true about herself but wondered if Curlygirl was just being overly sentimental about the whole thing. Ponyboy considered everyone's faith suspect—except for his own. Curlygirl wanted to punch him in the nose.

"⁹Blessed are the peacemakers," said the clown, *"for they shall be called children of God."*

"9. O the satisfaction of those who wangle right relationships between cowhands, for they are doing a Godlike work."

Ponyboy wondered if any of his relationships were right and pleasing to God. Perhaps the one with his horse. And here he was with an engagement ring in his pocket and nobody to give it to. At least he had left the box at home but the ring itself was too valuable to leave anywhere but in his pants or on a girl's finger. But not just any girl. Miss Jaycee had tried to make him drink that demon beer and who knows what other things she would want him to do—what other biblical standards she would want to tear down.

And Miss Curlygirl had gone over to Buck and done who knows what. It didn't take his mind long to fill in every detail. He felt rejected because he had high standards—clearly mistreated for his righteousness.

But wait, amazingly the clown was just now saying exactly that. The boy stopped gazing at Curlygirl's hair and tuned in again.

"*Matthew 5:[10]Blessed are those who are persecuted for **<u>righteousness</u>'** sake, for theirs is the kingdom of heaven.*"

The clown continued. "Now what if we try to unpack the meaning of the word righteousness? It means living in accordance with God's law and intensions. Right? And what would be the outward results of that? Wouldn't that display the fruit of the Spirit? And what are these fruits? Have a look at:

"*Galatians 5:[22]But the fruit of the Spirit is love, joy, peace, patience, kindness, goodness, faithfulness, [23]gentleness, self-control; against such things there is no law. [24]And those who belong to Christ Jesus have crucified the flesh with its passions and desires. [25]If we live by the Spirit, let us also keep in step with the Spirit. [26]Let us not become conceited, provoking one another, envying one another.*"

"So here is this last Beatitude in my own words. I've replaced the word 'righteousness' with the fruit of the Spirit.

"O hail to God's people victimized for their <u>love</u>, which uncovers hate in stark contrast.

"O hail to the Body of Christ resented for its <u>joy</u>, which reveals the despair of many.

"O hail to the Faithful attacked for their inner <u>peace</u>, so unlike their attackers who are angry at God.

"O hail to the Joint Heirs with Christ despised for their <u>patience</u>, which flies in the face of those intolerant of God.

"O hail to God's children punished for their <u>kindness</u> by those cruel to the weak and exploiting the helpless.

"O hail to the Saints of God reviled for their <u>goodness</u>, which challenges the forces of evil.

"O hail to God's sheep misunderstood for their <u>faithfulness</u>, and hated by the goats deserting God.

"O hail to the little lambs of God abused for their <u>gentleness</u>, which highlights aggressiveness and perversion.

"O hail to God's Church persecuted for its <u>self-control</u>, whose very life exposes the world's self-indulgence as sin."

The Bible study was over. Jaycee rushed out and bolted home like a mule to the barn. Ponyboy shuffled along, much as a hangdog with chocolate lips. As Curlygirl dawdled past him she brushed up near, just a little too close and hesitated just that split second on the steps. Their fate became sealed.

Already it was time to prepare for the evening's procession so Ponyboy made straight for the stall where Curlygirl kept her mount. After a short while she approached and found him lightly stroking the pretty mare's forehead.

"Are you ready for the parade?" she asked shyly, wondering what he was doing by her stall.

"Sure," he stammered, "but I have something for you first, if you'll have it." His mouth felt like it was full of cat litter. But diamonds sometimes give men confidence—only today not so much.

"Oh, I'll have most presents," she chirped, folding her hands and trying to keep things light. It was the first time they'd talked since the "great unpleasantness." She blushed recalling where her eyes and dreams had led lately. She didn't want to ruin everything again. Her tongue felt like a tennis ball.

"Will you have something like this?" he said, pulling the unwrapped ring out of his pocket and trying awkwardly to place it in her palm with thumb and forefinger. His hand felt like a lobster claw.

"Oh, my goodness," she gasped, jumping back, "is this real; is it a joke? Oh my gracious, is it a diamond? It's so big! What does this mean? Oh excuse me, I'm gunna be late for the parade." What an inglorious time it would be to throw up. Can you vomit for joy?

She grabbed her crucifix and her wide eyes blinked up into his. Oh if this was some awful trick she would just die—or kill someone. And isn't this a bit too bold, too daring, too improper? What does she really know about him? What are his motives? What about Jaycee? Curlygirl grabbed her heart. Deep down she knew she loved him, that's what. But this was too strange—and it was for the rest of her life.

His eyes told her he must be serious, if only in some misguided way. Her first inclination was to laugh in his face, but she'd made so many secret wishes upon the number pinned to his back that she hesitated just long enough to step off the cliff.

"May I answer you after the show?" she replied in a trembling voice.

"Of course," he said, weak kneed and steadying himself on her horse's neck. Both their faces turned a bright red. He made a hasty retreat before anything awful could happen.

She stared longingly, lovingly at the ring. It splashed light of every color imaginable into her eyes and yet when she looked directly at its center she could see straight into the deepest heart of happiness. Was she drooling? Quickly glancing around, she thrust it into her pants pocket. It was so big it made a noticeable bulge, even without a box, even in jeans. After saddling her horse, she took it out again and tried it on her finger. It fit just perfectly. Was this the measure of her worth to him? This much? But it was *too* much. He must have spent his entire savings on her. She felt privileged, pretty, proud. Even so, she took it off again and hid it back in her pocket. She could feel it on her thigh as she was guiding her horse into the main shoot. She was sure everyone watching the parade would be able to see the obvious bulge and would know everything it represented.

The music rose in piercing crescendos as the horses jostled in anticipation at the final gate. The girls on their backs took deep breaths and moistened their lips. Fingers grasped reins, knees and legs bumped. Anxious glances were exchanged through long eyelashes. Backs became straight then arched forward. At last the signal sounded and they were free and tearing around the arena in wild, spirited abandon. The silk flags crossed in and out and rode the wind like great birds. The horses kicked up turf in big clods and little girls in the first bleacher row shrieked in terror as they screamed by—tails

whipping the air behind them. The cowgirls were especially lively that day under the powerful lights and rays bounced bright from their sequined blouses and radiant eyes.

Curlygirl rode higher and happier than she had ever ridden in her life, for the ring in her pocket gave hope to her heart and wings to her soul. At last she was noticed. It was like she was flying. At last she was loved by someone who was not a rat.

So naturally when Buck roughly guided his big white stallion squarely beside her, and began to nudge her, she just sat there holding her flag even straighter and taller than usual. The cowboy's great nostrils flared like they did every day, and his arm waved grandly to the crowd. He again made a big show of tipping his hat to Jaycee on his left, and again swayed right in his saddle to inquire with the usual imposing flourish, "Will you marry me tonight, Chickabiddy?"

Shocked as always, she turned her head and averted her eyes. A blush appeared through the dust on her face. This day however, she was packed to bursting with confidence. She felt the ring through her pocket and then glared boldly up. "I'll trot down the aisle with you when horses fly!" she announced loud enough to reach even the top bleachers.

The remark felt delicious in her mouth. Like a chocolate covered cherry it buoyed her spirit. Sweet. Gooey. That is until she discovered the pit inside.

Chapter 8
The Judgment

The next day there was to be an evening rodeo, so the Bible study was early. It was 2 PM and Faithful was standing guard over Truth. In spite of her promise Curlygirl had not given Ponyboy an answer about his proposal. She still carried his ring, but in her pants not on her finger. Still they sat together and Jaycee was several seats away.

The clown was in an especially somber mood for some reason. "I am concerned that we don't know how to study our Bibles correctly." His words were measured and weighty. "When we come to a passage, first how do we understand it? I say when the plain meaning of Scripture makes common sense, take only that - with every word at its primary, ordinary, usual, literal sense, unless the facts of the immediate context, studied in light of related passages and axiomatic, fundamental truths, indicate clearly otherwise, or in the case of clearly figurative language, parables or types. Next, what questions do we bring to it? Do we ask, 'what is the meaning and how do I apply this to make me a better person?' Well that's fine as far as it goes, but that's entirely surface and man-centered. I've been thinking we should also be going deeper with, 'what does this tell me about God and his plans, and how do I fit in with them? How does this connect me with a holy God? Worship his majesty?' This is a God-centered approach, which is so much better."

Everyone sitting in the circle seemed to be nodding their heads, but more in the fashion of bobble-head dolls than understanding adults.

"Here," continued the clown, "I've made my own little tool for interacting with God's overarching theme found in the Bible. As you are reading the Bible ask yourself two questions:

1. How does this Scripture passage illustrate:

    A. Only God is sovereign.
    B. Only Christ surpasses all creation, (concrete and abstract).
    C. Only Christians are joint heirs with him in his eternal kingdom.

2. How will I reflect this in my heart & life?"

"For example, *John 3:16-17, 'For God so loved the world, that he gave his only Son, that whoever believes in him should not perish but have eternal life. For God did not send his Son into the world to condemn the world, but in order that the world might be saved through him.'*

"Only a sovereign God could grant eternal life and it is only through faith in Christ that I'm saved by him into his eternal kingdom. Rejoicing and praising God for this spills out of me.

"*Psalm 19:14, 'Let the words of my mouth and the meditation of my heart be acceptable in your sight, O LORD, my rock and my redeemer.'*

"A rock is strong and steadfast—qualities of a sovereign. Only Christ is my true redeemer. Therefore I can't help but seek to please him in all my thoughts and speech."

After this was a brief discussion of the seven churches in *Revelation 2 and 3*. Soon it was as if the Word of God was speaking from God—which it always does. As he looked around the room the clown remarked, "You know, I think I might have something important to say to each of you stemming straight from Christ in this material." Without stopping for comment he said:

"1. Ephesus was the church that abandoned its first love (*Revelation 2:1-7*). Curlygirl, you love Jesus so much but I have this against you. Your love for Christ is strong but shallow and you have left even that, your first love to worship men and their abilities on horseback. I hope you therefore will serve Christ by serving one man only, bearing and raising many children. Your calling is weighty but your burden is bearable. Christ's yoke is easy as you share it with him.

"2. Smyrna was the church that would be persecuted (*Revelation 2:8-11*). Some here will share in this, including me. I pray for us in this special blessing.

"3. Pergamum was the church that needed to repent (*Revelation 2:12-17*). Ponyboy, you love your Bible so much but I have this against you. It's not how much you mark your Bible but how much your Bible marks you. Flitting from one girl to another smacks of sexual immorality. Your calling is to lay down your life for one woman. I trust you will fight heresy all your life. May the Bible be your sword.

"4. Thyatira was the church with the false prophetess (*Revelation 2:18-29*). Some of you will follow Christian fakes and fads all your lives. May you not fade as others do.

"5. Sardis was the church that was about to die (*Revelation 3:1-6*). Will this Bible study suffer the same fate? We will soon find out.

"6. Philadelphia was the church that endured patiently (*Revelation 3:7-13*). Every remnant seems small, doesn't it? Yet they are precious to God and the fabric of his true church.

"7. Laodicea was the lukewarm church (*Revelation 3:14-22*). Oh Jaycee, you love people so much but I have this against you. You do not love Christ as much. You are neither hot nor cold so he spits you out of his mouth. Your god is too small. But Jaycee I pray you will become Christ's own special bride for a life of single-minded service and reward on behalf of him. You don't need a man to save you, just the Son of Man. Your calling is high but your burden will be light. You will soar on wings of eagles, but you will fly alone, except that Christ will be with you always. And that will be enough. Your God is always more than enough."

Everyone at the Bible study had to confess that not everything made complete sense. Several were shaking their heads, but others were bowing theirs.

The clown continued, "We are living under grace, the completely unmerited favor of God, but when our eyes lead us into extravagant relationship contexts and wishful encounter scenarios, then we are sinning into each other's fantasies. May we seek instead the deeper and more lasting joy that comes only from reality—the Savior and what he provides. How does this joy come? Foremost by considering what Christ has done for us. What has he done? Well everything. First he created our progenitors. Then he prepared a lovely estate in which to live. In it he bestowed the beauty of landscapes, the serenity and practicality of gardens, and the companionship of animals. Then he imparted this even more lavishly in relationships with each other, male and female, then children. He planted meaning and significance into our lives and we communed with him richly. But later we rebelled and disobeyed his simple command. This brought his just and terrible curse upon ourselves and all creation. We became wicked and wandered helpless, exalting none but ourselves, compelling him to cleanse the world with a flood. But still we chose evil. So he selected one man to be his own. He gave this man a family, nurtured them on fertile ground, then put them under the special protection of a great nation so they might safely increase in numbers and grow strong. When that country enslaved them, God led them into the wilderness to forge their own nation. By his might they conquered a new land which he promised them forever. But still they vacillated between rebellion and repentance, so God instituted a royal dynasty from which would come their King of kings and Lord of lords. Periodically God sent special men and angels to tell them about himself and his will. But they rarely listened or obeyed, so he sent great pagan empires to carry them off into captivity. Eventually God permitted a return to their own land so that this High King could be born as predicted. It was this Christ who paid the price for their disobedience. He did this hanging on a death cross and today his blood covers every tribe and nation—those of us he brings into salvation. We are undeserving but he is love. And his love conquers all, even death. Yet *still* some of us refuse him. So these choose to remain forever separated from him in hell's torment. But we believers remain eternally secure with him in heaven's joy. That's why I love him so. So why would you abandon this great everlasting adoration to fight among yourselves in vile worldly lust, making graven idols out of each other? Are not such objects deceitful pleasure, patently inferior and ultimately fleeting?"

The crackers and cheese began to stick in everyone's craw. Coffee rippled in unsteady cups. Eyes hid in Bibles or folded hands. Some people rose to leave. But the clown wasn't finished. "Instead of the false freedom of abused grace that leads to licentiousness—extravagant immorality—even to the point of an unbiblical church hierarchy committing unspeakable sexual perversions—why don't we seek the surpassing joy of God's love?" An atmosphere of gloom had fallen everywhere as finally everyone began shuffling out past Faithful.

But the seeds of truth had been sown and immediately began to germinate. Only the Holy Spirit changes hearts and some were already starting to yield under his perfect will.

The next day Curlygirl noticed that Ponyboy was not entered in the calf roping event. Soon after that her concern turned to gloom when she observed the mighty Buck flying after a calf on Ponyboy's magical horse. Of course the horse performed beautifully and of course Buck with all his superior strength and bravado was able to smash the rodeo record every time he left the chute. Also smashing was his showmanship before the crowd. His teeth positively gleamed. Also smashing were her hopes for the future—for she knew then what Ponyboy had done. He had traded his only horse for the ring in her pocket. It hardly seemed something a sane person would do.

Next morning she was pounding on his door before the sun rays did. She stormed in. "Even if you do love me," she railed, "how do you expect to support us with no horse? Do you expect us to live on left-over popcorn? Do you expect to win prize money riding my pretty pony? Do you expect me to get rich for us waving a flag around and losing the barrel race to that Jaycee every day? Didn't your daddy tell you not to let your yearnings get ahead of your earnings!"

"I thought we could make it on love," came his trite and muffled reply.

"Yeah, but making love makes youngins, not money, so you'll have to make it alone, Lone Ranger. I'll be hot to trot with you when horses fly!" She was barking cruelly, but in a breaking voice. Reluctantly she closed his fingers around the ring and gave him a parting peck on the cheek, which he didn't return. It was her first kiss ever onto the face of a man.

Chapter 9
The Ransom

Ponyboy felt like a crazy wet cat. He took off racing in his truck—for no rational reason and in no determined direction. What did his life amount to anyway? Not a pile of pinto beans. He owned his clothes and precious else precious. A cheap saddle, a bridle but the bank owned everything of value. He'd no horse certainly. Beside him on the seat was not a honeybunch bride, but a baloney sandwich, and he wasn't hungry. Next to it was his Bible, but he wasn't thirsty. At that moment even "living water" seemed like bilge. Life is but a poem we write to God. Was his full of love or anger—joy or shame. He was finding it hard to drive through the tears flooding his face.

But wait—the *ring!* Just then he remembered how he'd acquired it in the first place. He remembered the agreement. He remembered the midnight deadline. It was already eleven PM. If he could get that useless thing back to Buck before twelve the deal would be off. He'd just one hour to get back and find him. But that wasn't enough time. So what! Ponyboy turned his rig around and tore out as if chasing a calf. He brought new meaning to the term "speed limit" and new definitions to "stop sign" and "red light." And yes, his faithful Ford did land him in front of Buck's place just 10 minutes before midnight.

Buck took nine of those to get out of bed. He was not as lively as at a party. He was slow as snails. But just before the last clock chime Ponyboy was able to slap the ring down on the table directly beneath Buck's flaring nostrils. "Deal's off," Ponyboy said.

"Whoa pardner," answered Buck, veins standing out on his neck. "Our midnight's well passed. The horse is still mine."

"No, the clock chimed just now. You heard," Ponyboy said.

"Sure, that was the next midnight after our deal," said Buck. "A day begins with midnight. So you're a day late, my boy. Your deadline was twenty-four hours ago. The horse's mine forever. So pick up that ring and get your skinny tail outta here. By the way, what happened?" he added, glancing at the ring, "you come up short with her?"

With this Ponyboy grabbed the ring and in his blurry rage to run also grabbed a revolver off the wall. There were pistols in every nook and cranny.

"Hey, that shooter's loaded!" Buck yelled after him. But Ponyboy was deaf to anything but fury. All Buck's guns were always loaded and ready for action.

Ponyboy headed straight for the clown who told him that midnight on a certain day technically means the start of that day, which clicks over at the stroke of 12. "Yet when most people speak of it," he continued, "they mean the end of that present day, say 11:59. So? It's ambiguous. But is it necessary to get this information from me at gunpoint?"

Ponyboy glanced down at the weapon pointed at his friend, paled and then bolted out into the woods like a varmint—pistol in one hand, ring in the other, and stumbling, grumbling over sticks and stones. Falling on a loaded gun would be a bad idea and especially when the safety is off. Buck always kept his safeties off and ready for anything. Ponyboy didn't really know what a safety was.

The clown looked anxiously out the door after him but the boy was running like a crazed rabbit. He was zigzagging as if pursued by some furious fox—if only in his mind. But our minds are the stages upon which we must act. Soon he was out of sight, so the gentle man pulled on his boots, prayed briefly, then headed over to Buck's. Before reaching for the horseshoe knocker he reached for his cellphone.

"Dad," he muttered in a broken voice, "I realize we talked about this before, but I really don't want to do it. You know that. Isn't there any other way? It seems such a steep price to pay. Almost reckless. Can any one person be that important really?" There was a long pause, then, "Yes I know it's not a payment to Buck, but a ransom to satisfy your fairness and justice. Yes sure, of course Father, I can see your mind. So be it. We'll do it your way. As always. Your way is my way. It's our way." Another pause, then. "I love you too Dad. Thank you for sending me here." He shut off the phone and shoved it back into his pocket. A single tear flowed slowly across his cheek and onto his gentle smile, almost as if he were still in conversation with his father. It seemed he was always with his father in spirit. Yet even closer than that somehow.

The knock at the door broke rudely into Buck's regained serenity and forced him out of bed again. The big man grabbed a gun fearing Ponyboy might be returning with less than serene intensions. Buck was half dressed, hairy legs evident and grossly mammalian. His head hair was a category four hurricane as was the brain underneath. His eyes were the funnels of twin cyclones.

"What the devil!" he said flinging open the door, a big black pistol where a handshake should be.

The clown brushed it aside nonchalantly and entered. "Is it necessary to greet your visitors at gunpoint?" he inquired.

Buck returned it to a wall and explained. "Ponyboy has gone plumb loco. He stole a piece and skedaddled like a hare on fire. I hope he doesn't attack anyone with it."

"Yes, I just saw him," said the clown, "he wanted to return your ring and get his horse back."

"I know," said Buck, "he wasn't man enough for Curlygirl."

At this remark the clown stared into his eyes until they settled sufficiently to absorb this next statement. He went on, "I know who is a man and who was not man enough for Curlygirl even when he tried to force himself on her with bad medicine. Appears you needed medicine too. I can see your mind, my friend."

This extinguished the storms around Buck and he pulled in his countenance like a whipped dog. For all his blow and bluster, he was nothing but bluff.

"But I would like to propose a new deal," said the clown, "I will buy that horse from you."

Buck cocked his head contemptuously. "Aha, but you see," he said, "that horse is precious to me because it wins me races. You can't put a price on that, so no sale. Besides it keeps it out of Ponyboy's hands and that gives me a chance for the all-around championship and also with Curlygirl."

"You are essentially running this rodeo now, aren't you?" said the clown.

"Yes, you don't see the owner objecting, do you?" asked Buck.

"Well how would you like to own it outright?" the clown asked.

"You know I ain't got that kind of dough," said Buck.

"You have that horse."

"You mean a trade, the whole rodeo kit and caboodle for a single horse?"

"Exactly."

"That's crazy, besides the owner'd never go for it."

With this, the clown presented a bill of sale marked "paid in full." It was made out to Buck and signed by the owner.

"But this has you as previous owner," said Buck.

"That's right, I'm the owner of this rodeo, but I'll trade it right now for Ponyboy's horse."

Buck thought it too good to be true but grabbed the paper at once and signed it with a wobbly hand. "Go get the stupid nag," he said, "he's yours. And then kindly get off my property."

Chapter 10
The Gift

The clown headed into the woods, carefully leading Ponyboy's horse. The night hid everything mysteriously but a naked moon danced for them from behind tall, swaying trees. Every darting shadow seemed creature-like and every rock a hole from which could crawl evil, black creatures, all eyes, teeth and claws. The crack of sticks and rustle of leaves under their feet played into fears. Anxiety became fear and fear, blind trust. They appeared lost, but when the clown jumped on bareback the horse seemed to know where to find his master. They quickly abandoned the roadways and followed deer trails which slip through the trees as friends.

Before long they approached a small clearing where a forlorn cowboy could be seen sitting on a log slowly rotating the cylinder of a blue-black pistol. Click click click it went as if ticking off time. His head was bowed, his knees apart, and his feet pidgin-toed. His boot uppers were separating from their soles. His eyes were buried beneath the brim of a black baseball cap. Tick tick tick, he hardly seemed worth the great price of his impending ransom. But what value can be put on love?

The clown slid gracefully from Ponyboy's horse and approached him slowly. The horse followed, nickered softly, then nudged the boy's baseball cap off to the ground. Ponyboy appeared irritated and still gripping the pistol, buried his head in his hands. The horse pricked his ears, then nuzzled his master's shoulder.

"Please take Buck's horse away," Ponyboy said.

"He's not Buck's horse anymore, he's mine," said the clown.

"What?"

"That's right. He's mine," said the clown, "I bought him at great price and now I'd love to give him to you."

"I can't pay," said Ponyboy.

"It's a free gift," said the clown.

"Oh wait, I've a ring in my pocket," said Ponyboy, "take that."

The clown looked sternly into his dark face, "There's nothing you have that can buy this horse, but you can accept it as a gift. Or reject it."

Ponyboy still had the gun in his hands. He stared at it. "Look what I've turned into," he said. "I was going to take my own life. I'm finished. Down deep I'm nothing but a sinner. I've abandoned even God. I don't deserve such a gift."

"I know you don't," said the clown, "but it's free to you. You're not worthy to receive it but I'm worthy to give it. All you have to do is take these reins."

Ponyboy looked up at his horse and then flung himself around its neck. It was easy as that, easy as stroking its mane and whispering in its ear. Soon the two men were riding double. Out of the woods they came and into camp. The sun was just beginning to rise and was the size of a giant fireball fixing to set the forest ablaze. Ponyboy dropped the clown off and headed directly over to Curlygirl's. His heart felt like it was bursting and burning.

He knocked a bit too hard perhaps, but jumped clear to the ground this time when the door finally flung open. Curlygirl was in shorty pink panther pajamas and her hair was abounding in blond frenzy. Her eyes however, were crouching behind heavy lids.

She wanted to say something witty and endearing but "Did you steal that horse back?" was all that came out.

"It's my salvation," he said, "and it's a free gift from God. I didn't even have to pay for it."

"Buck will kill you," she said.

"Buck no longer owns it," he said, "I do."

"Well if that's so, then tie it up, and come in for some breakfast," she said.

Ten minutes later she was returning to the table with some hash and eggs. He told her to sit and without appropriate fanfare, slapped the ring down under her cute button nose. He was trying to be romantic, but remember he was nevertheless a cowboy.

"You have **both** the horse **and** the ring," she exclaimed, looking up into his face.

"No, I have the horse and you'll have the ring," he said with a satisfied smile.

She blushed. "I'll have the ring," she said, "if you'll have me."

"Me and my horse," he said.

"*And* if you'll get down on one knee—or at least sit down on this chair."

Well that was it. They embraced and kissed briefly before the eggs got cold. No, that was not it at all. The eggs were very cold indeed before they were ever noticed again.

Chapter 11
The Wedding

Like two trees growing entwined in enduring harmony Ponyboy and Curlygirl decreed that their wedding ceremony would forever be a portrait of their lives. Consequently it would be held in prelude to an actual rodeo performance. If they did it after the rodeo they would be too dirty.

That day the show started like every other—with a parade. Being special it was more like a procession. First in rode Ponyboy and a minister dressed like a circuit rider from old Dodge City. He wore a big black hat and a white clerical collar. The only thing he carried was an oversized Bible, barely noticeable against his dark outfit. Ponyboy must have been wearing a rented costume because it was more elaborate than anything he had ever worn in his life. It featured natural rhinestone crystals in intricate designs, elegant gold plated buttons, fringes everywhere, and decorative chaps. His boots were all leather with fancy tassels, pointed toes and high, angled "cowboy" heels. He sat tall in the saddle but his face was drained of color. He wore a real cowboy hat and it was white as snow. Snow. He wondered if he could be in too deep and if it was too late to light out on his back trail. But at least his horse seemed confident in demeanor and gait.

Next in was Buck prancing beside Jaycee. She was absolutely striking in her pure white buckskin tunic and leggings. These were decorated with ermine tails, hair, and intricate red and blue quillwork. The quills were from prickly porcupines. Some of the hair looked disturbingly like human scalps, but never mind that; they were old. On her feet were high-top milky white moccasins with fancy red flowers embroidered. These matched the design of her headband which was a deerskin strip beaded with tribal designs. It held a single tall egret feather proudly above her head. The entire outfit matched her horse blanket which was red and white with fringes reaching almost to the ground. Everything contrasted starkly with her long black hair which she wore in two girlish braids. Across her lap she carried an old hickory handled tomahawk. Word had it that her great-grandfather had pulled it from the back of a Union cavalry officer. There was a pipe-bowl forged into the metal head and the shaft was drilled for smoking. Thus it could either be a pipe of peace or an axe of war.

Every so often she held it high and as the crowd gasped, her eyes glistened like stars and her smile far outshined everything in the arena. Everything that is except Buck's white teeth which he deftly displayed to one and all. Oh that Buck. It looked like he had diamonds mounted into his hat and his spurs were solid gold. Clinging to his hips were two massive polished pistols fully loaded with silver bullets, one would presume. When Jaycee raised her tomahawk he would brandish them in double response. He tried to reach over and hug the Indian princess but she gave him the classic stiff-arm in response. This drew a ripple of murmur from the crowd. So Buck wheeled his horse to the right to join Ponyboy and Jaycee swung to the left. The battle was over. Ponyboy eyed Buck. He would have preferred the clown as his best man but he didn't want to argue with two Colt 45s, whatever they were loaded with.

After this the other rodeo riders entered in pairs, boy with girl as wedding attendants. Each couple was dressed in matching Western attire and paced their mounts in expert dressage—a synchronized horse ballet of love. The men rode stiff and strong as the women smiled and blew kisses to the crowd. Couples in the bleachers began holding hands and little girls blushed. Boys feigned disinterest.

The last pair was something of a spectacle and overshadowed everything previous. The clown rode in next. Since there was to be a rodeo immediately following the ceremony, and because it takes hours to apply clown makeup, he was fully dressed right down to his baggy pants and big red nose. He rode his white Faithful.

Beside him and beaming was the bride Curlygirl. Her dress was purity white and flowing everywhere. Its lace was wispy and studded Western style with rubies, sapphires and diamonds. Real ones could not have looked any better. Its train was so long it covered her horse's rump and tail right down to the ground. She looked like a medieval princess. Crowning her golden curls was the whisper of a cloudlike veil which brought out her eyes like bright morning stars. Around her neck was her silver cross and on her finger the sparkling ring. Her wedding shoes were tall cowgirl boots of white tooled leather. On her lap she carried an ample bouquet of colorful sage flowers. All happy daisies that said, "He loves me!"

"My fellow ranch hands," began the minister as they reached the middle of the arena, "we are gathered here to hitch this here cowpoke and this here cowgirl in holy matrimony. Who gives this woman to this man?"

"I do," the clown said. It was the first time the crowd had ever heard him speak. He leaned from his saddle to hug the bride so she let him, getting some crimson makeup on her veil. Stiff-arms had to be employed once more as they strained to sit erect in their saddles again. Amazingly all was done with calm dignity. The clown then took his place well behind the preacher and almost out of the picture. Yet from this position he could silently oversee everything. Somehow even with his silly painted-on grin he commanded respect from all present. Some people were even afraid of him.

Curlygirl's hands began to shake as she gazed into the clown's decorated eyes. It made her flowers dance nervously. She wondered, "Wow, what have I been doing? I've been trading in my desire for Jesus for man-hankering. She noticed Buck's well-defined pectorals through his shirt. How can I possibly be the Bride of the Lamb when I'm so preoccupied with beef?" She grabbed her cross and clung to it over her heart.

Buck appeared bored. He gazed into the sky, whipped out his cellphone and took a selfie picture for Facebook. He had 2681 friends there. Then another pic next to his best buddy forever, his right bicep. His horse pawed the turf. Next, in a booming voice he interrupted the proceedings with, "Aw shucks, let's git on with it. Do you puny Ponyboy here take this Bubblicious stick of honey gum to be your lawful bedded wife, to have and to hold, and to chew on from this day forward? Amen?" He looked over at the crowd and there were cries of amused assent. "And you Sweet Breathmint, do ya take this worthless sack of cheap chewin' tobacci to live between yer cheek and gum fer ever 'till spittin' time?"

The couple, caught off guard muttered something but nobody heard them. I suppose it mattered little since few vows are strictly kept nowadays, if at all.

"If anyone objects," Buck continued, "they can jest stay seated or have a parlay with my twin peacemakers here. See? Now both of yous repeat after me."

"We're crazy but we takes each other to enjoy, train and manage somehow so long as we both shall love."

98

At this the real minister stepped in and glancing away from Buck, pronounced somewhat sheepishly, "I'm sure you will love, honor and cherish each other as well as can be expected in this day and age, and since it's past time for the show to start, so by the authority vested in me I now pronounce you husband and wife. –Yes, it's legal."

It all happened so fast the now married couple was quite caught off guard. They eyed each other. Obviously no one expected a kiss on horseback but his eyes were pleading and hers were longing. So throwing caution to the wind they leaned then toppled onto each other, embraced and kissed. Their horses, being rodeo trained stood still for this, although it was quite new to them. It was new to the riders as well and pleasurable as it might be, they weren't sure how to extricate themselves. Stiff arms weren't working, so Curlygirl raised her left leg over her saddle and pushed off hard with her knee. She did this with such force that her right leg swung around in the air, landing her upright on Ponyboy's horse and tightly in his arms facing him. Her own horse fled in terror. Ponyboy had to slip back in his saddle to get her off the horn. Her legs were around his waist but you couldn't exactly tell because of her voluminous outfit. She yanked at it but only succeeded in covering the horse's head. This started him into running but Ponyboy managed to scoop everything up around them cocoon-like. The ample train covered both their heads and the horse's as well. Still Ponyboy could see through it well enough to guide them around the arena in a couple of wild victory laps. The crowd, thinking it all part of the act, erupted in laughter and clapping, then boot stomping. It was the best Wild West event seen in those parts since Buffalo Bill and Annie Oakley. But Curlygirl was absolutely horrified.

While this was happening the wedding party brought out a giant wedding cake on a tiny clown cart. It was a carrot cake topped with the red ribbon bow from Curlygirl's hat. It was ringed like sunbeams with whole carrots, two for each horse in attendance. On the rear of the cart were their felt rodeo back numbers taped side by side. 12 and 7 coincidentally. She was such a tiny girl she couldn't wear a double digit number. Then the attendant riders circled the railing tossing donut holes to everyone from big buckets.

Now maybe this doesn't seem like a real wedding, but bear in mind that donut holes aren't really holes either. Not everything in the story of life is as it seems on the surface. Yet determining truth can be as easy as looking up *John 14:6*.

The horse-camp honeymoon made a fitting consummation to these events, especially with Faithful tagging along as pack horse.

Time passed and legend has it throughout the entire rodeo circuit that they became famous and lived happily ever after. As for Buck he continued running the rodeo and it truly became a Wild West show with sharpshooters, exotic animals and dancing girls. There was even an elephant which no one really knew what to do with. It just walked around like an elephant. Everyone wore a gun, but only loaded with blanks. Buck did most of the blustering and bragging, especially with women but everyone knew he was shooting blanks. He was quite impotent. Still he took to carrying real bullets in his pants instead of jewelry, and was clever in his use of them.

The Bible studies continued, but led by Ponyboy and his wife. Curlygirl started marking up her Bible and it became quite messy. Yet the Jesus on the outside didn't mind one bit. Much was learned about God and man, but curiously no one ever found out their real names, this shy Ponyboy and his sparkly eyed Curlygirl.

I know but I'll never tell.

Epilogue
When Horses Fly

My dear reader perhaps you're wondering what became of Jaycee, the raven-haired Native girl. She never married. I suppose she would have been a bit hard to handle. Still, God made her life rich beyond all measure. Marriage is great, a symbol of Christ and his Church, but some are called to an equally high purpose, an excellent one—single-minded union with Christ himself. With this she became a great and fruitful soldier for God on a whole different plane. Have you ever approached such people and said, "Thank you for your service?" And in addition, what husband could ever say he created a special, beautiful landscape just to stroll alone in with his bride? Her hand-in-hand romance with Jesus is great because he adores her passionately and perfectly plans quiet, alone times with her in places she loves. All she needs do is submit to this sweet communion—and she does. It's a big big love because he is infinite, indivisible and all hers.

Now what of the truthful clown in the end? He had sacrificed his beloved rodeo for Ponyboy, the poorest of riders and in doing so elevated Buck, the most despicable to Ruler of This World. (*John 12:31*) Does this make any sense to you at all? Yes, the clown left the rodeo and it was as if he went into hiding. Actually he went to be with his father for a while and became his right-hand man so to speak. What a good and beloved son he was. So what else happened to the clown? Well for one thing people discovered he had all sorts of descriptive names, but they never uncovered them all. You can find them if you look. They also found out that the end while near, has yet to arrive. So how can it be recounted properly here? Therefore the best thing perhaps is to have you read the following passages from God's own hand through a man named John. You may follow it to make your own conclusions to this story.

"Revelation 19:11-16

The Rider on a White Horse
[11]Then I saw heaven opened, and behold, a white horse! The one sitting on it is called Faithful and True, and in righteousness he judges and makes war. [12]His eyes are like a flame of fire, and on his head are many diadems, and he has a name written that no one knows but himself. [13]He is clothed in a robe dipped in blood, and the name by which he is called is The Word of God. [14]And the armies of heaven, arrayed in fine linen, white and pure, were following him on white horses. [15]From his mouth comes a sharp sword with which to strike down the nations, and he will rule them with a rod of iron. He will tread the winepress of the fury of the wrath of God the Almighty. [16]On his robe and on his thigh he has a name written,

King of kings and Lord of lords."

By the way, are you wondering about Buck at all? Read on.

"Revelation 20:10

The Defeat of Satan
[10]*and the devil who had deceived them was thrown into the lake of fire and sulfur, ... tormented day and night forever and ever."*

In the end Buck had no recourse but to cry out to God. But he had one difficulty. He himself was his god.

Yes, the End Times are near and as you know, this will truly be the time "when horses fly."

www.ingramcontent.com/pod-product-compliance
Lightning Source LLC
Chambersburg PA
CBHW031519040426
42445CB00009B/305